Kittens know
they're cute.
Always.

Napping is better
with a friend.

Life with a cat is always
full of surprises.

The

CAT
lover

The Best Experts' Advice for a
Happy, Healthy Cat with Stories and
Photos of Fabulous Felines

Marty Becker, D.V.M.
Gina Spadafori
Carol Kline
Mikkel Becker

Health Communications, Inc.
HCI Books, the Life Issues Publisher
Deerfield Beach, Florida

www.hcibooks.com
www.ultimatehcibooks.com

We would like to acknowledge the writers and photographers who granted us permission to use their material. Copyright credits for interior photographs appear on each photograph and credits for literary work are listed alphabetically by authors' last names. Contact information as supplied by the photographers and writers can be found in the back matter of this book.

In Their Own Way. © Sabrina Abercromby. All rights reserved.
¡Caliente! © Marty Becker. All rights reserved.
Lost? . . . and Found Quickly! © Liz Blackman. All rights reserved.

(*Copyright credits continued on page 246*)

**Library of Congress Cataloging-in-Publication Data
is available through the Library of Congress.**

©2008 Marty Becker, Gina Spadafori, Carol Kline, Mikkel Becker
ISBN-13: 978-0-7573-0751-5
ISBN-10: 0-7573-0751-5

Publisher: Health Communications, Inc.
            3201 S.W. 15th Street
            Deerfield Beach, FL 33442-8190

Cover Design: Larissa Hise Henoch
Cover Photo: ©Photographer: Rafal Glebowski / Agency: Dreamstime.com
Photo Editor: Justin Rotkowitz
Interior Design: Lawna Patterson Oldfield
Inside Formatting: Dawn Von Strolley Grove

*We dedicate this book to every cat who
lavishes gifts on a human family.*

*To the families who make sure their cats' health
and happiness is a priority.*

*To all members of the veterinary healthcare team
and everyone involved with animal treatment,
rescue, and rehabilitation.*

*To all healthcare providers who harness
the healing power of pets to improve
human health and well-being.*

*To the special love of cats as celebrated
in stories, photographs, memories,
and heartfelt emotions.*

*And finally to God for the gift of animals and the
life-affirming bond we share with them.*

Is something "Ultimately" important to you?
Then we want to know about it. . . .

We hope you enjoyed *The Ultimate Cat Lover*. We are planning many more books in the Ultimate series, each filled with entertaining stories, must-know facts, and captivating photos. We're always looking for talented writers to share slice-of-life true stories, creative photographers to capture images that a story can't tell, as well as top experts to offer their unique insights on a given topic.

For more information on submission guidelines, or to suggest a topic for an upcoming book, please visit the Ultimate website at **www.ultimatehcibooks.com**, or write to: Submission Guidelines, Ultimate Series, HCI Books, 3201 SW 15th St., Deerfield Beach, FL 33442.

For more information about other books by Health Communications, Inc., please visit **www.hcibooks.com**.

Contents

celebrating the Bond

Feline Love

Feline Mayhem, Mischief, and Mystery

Must-Know Info

Introduction

Of all the animals who have shared our lives for generations, we know the least about the cat.

That doesn't mean we love them any less; in fact, the air of mystery each cat carries is one of the reasons we love them so much. Cats have never changed to suit our desires. They play by their own rules, and we love and admire them for their independence of spirit.

Cats started hanging around with us because we were useful to them. Our switch from hunter-gatherers to farmers meant that we attracted lots of fat, little rodents to our grain stores. The cat has been welcome in our barns ever since, and by our hearths as well.

Few cats have to earn their living today, and many now have lives that keep them completely indoors, hunting for little beyond a warm place to sleep. More than twenty years have passed since the cat claimed the title of number-one pet over the dog, and the gap just keeps widening.

The closer we get to our cats, the more we find to love about them. Their company offers warm companionship, endless entertainment, and soothing comfort. Even science has documented the benefits: Pets in general, and cats in particular, are good for us in countless ways. They keep us busy, keep us from being lonely, and even help keep us healthier.

Those of us whose hearts are in this book are unabashed animal lovers. Animals are our lives, and it shows in the work we have chosen—whether as veterinarians, writers, or photographers. We cannot imagine living without them. We love cats, from the purr of a new kitten's greeting to the last sad good-bye of an aged friend. We love the snuggles on the couch while watching TV, the silly games with a string toy or laser pointer, the sharing of a joke or a secret or even a little bit of our dinner. Our cats are always with us, in spirit even when they cannot be with us in person.

We know we are not alone in the appreciation of all things feline. Every cat lover knows cats don't care who you are or what you look like. They love us, regardless.

Cats teach us, heal us, make us laugh, and break our hearts with their passing. We understand the benefits of feline companionship because we live with cats, love them, and care for and about them. Our lives are about helping others to find better, fuller lives with their pets. The strength of the human-animal bond and the growing importance of pets in our lives is why we wanted to compile this book.

The very best experts—including top veterinarians, trainers, behaviorists—were tapped to provide expertise on all manner of feline topics, but we wanted much, much more. We knew cat lovers had stories of feline love, loyalty, laughter, rescue, and courage, and we knew we wanted to share them, along with pictures that captured their varied personalities, magnificent beauty, and irresistable charm.

From thousands of submissions of stories and photographs, we have chosen the very best—the ones we loved, and the ones we hope you'll love, too. Please join us as we celebrate the cat.

Acknowledgments

I takes a talented team working behind the scenes to make the magic in a book happen. There are dozens of people, each with a specific niche, who brought *The Ultimate Cat Lover* from conception, to creation, to its place on your favorite booksellers' shelves.

Our biggest thank-you goes to our cats—past and present—for their patience while we learned how to love, nurture, and care for them, and appreciation for them letting us into their world.

Thank you to everyone who submitted their stories and photographs for consideration. While we were only able to use a small portion of the thousands of stories and photographs that were sent in, we know that each word and picture came from a heartfelt place.

This book would not have been possible without the generosity of some of the world's top veterinarians, behaviorists, trainers, breeders, and other experts who dedicate their careers to making life better for pets and people. You'll find all you need to know about these talented professionals following each of the "Must-Know Info" topics in which they share their expertise.

We especially thank our publisher, Peter Vegso, who believes in us and supports us in a myriad of ways, for publishing our last eight consecutive pet books. With HCI Books there is harmony, joy, trust, flexibility, excitement, experience, professionalism, can-do-ism, and a shared love of both pets and people. We tip our hats in sincere appreciation and respect to every member of the HCI team whose efforts allow us to show these books off with pride!

We owe a huge amount of gratitude and love to our story editor, Cindy Buck, whose enormous talent and commitment are only rivaled by the beauty of her heart, mind, and spirit. Cindy, we couldn't have done it without you—nor would we have wanted to.

On a more personal level, we simply cannot do what we do without the support of our families and friends.

Marty wishes to thank his beloved wife Teresa, son Lex, daughter Mikkel, and son-in-law Pat, for their love and support. The Becker family shares Almost Heaven Ranch in northern Idaho with a menagerie of four-legged family members—dogs, cats, and horses—that are a constant source of joy. Worthy of special mention is his colleague, mentor, and friend, Dr. R. K. Anderson, one of the cofounders of the Delta Society, a world-renowned veterinary behaviorist, and inventor, and the founder of ABRIonline.org.

Gina's love and appreciation goes out to her brother Joe, who is her very best friend, and her parents, Louise and Nino, her brother Pete, his wife, Sally, and their bright and talented children, Kate and Steven. Thanks to Christie Keith and Morgan Ong, friends who are really family. And, of course, to all the animals who continue to teach the lessons of love and acceptance.

Carol thanks her husband, Larry, who is the love of her life and who not only makes it possible for her to spend all of her time writing and editing, but makes it all worthwhile. Thanks also to her wonderful stepchildren, Lorin and McKenna, and to her mother, Selma, brothers Jim and Burt, and sisters Barbara and Holly, and their families, for being her favorite people in the world. Big belly rubs and lots of w-a-l-k-s for dogs Beau, Beethoven, and Jimmy-pop, and perennial love and fascination for the cats of the world.

Mikkel foremost wants to thank God for his love and blessings. Her dearly loved husband, Pat, never ceases to make her laugh and keep her life full with his on-the-edge spontaneity and fun, while her children (pugs), Willy and Bruce, keep her entertained with their wrestling and cuddling. And special thanks to her family cheerleaders, who have shared her accomplishments and achievements: Marty, Teresa, Lex, Valdie, Rockey, Virginia, Joan, Pete, Mike, and Joanie, for their enduring love and support.

Marty Becker
Gina Spadafori
Carol Kline
Mikkel Becker

Teachers and Healers

Love Pats

By Mitzi Flyte

I t was the call I'd hoped would never come.

At 5:00 AM, the phone rang. Rich, the man I was to marry, was at the University of Pennsylvania Hospital waiting for a heart transplant, and I was staying at a nearby hotel. Rich had recently had complications, so this early-morning phone call could mean only one thing. He was gone.

I'd been divorced almost seven years when I met Rich, a burly policeman. He'd had one heart attack years before and was not taking care of himself—he loved beer and could eat a hoagie while waiting for the pizza to bake. As a nurse I tried to encourage better habits, and for a while it seemed to be working. But the damage had already been done.

One heart attack followed another. The policeman who once weighed 230 pounds was down to 160. But his eyes still lit up whenever he saw me, and I hung on to that love.

When he finally became too weak to be at home, he was admitted to the cardiac care unit and given intravenous medication just to keep his heart working. There was only one option left: Rich would need a heart transplant. I papered his hospital room wall with a poster of a tropical isle—where we would honeymoon. We waited and waited. Then there were complications, and the doctors said that he wouldn't survive surgery. We would just have to wait until the complications cleared, and *then* he'd have his new heart.

But he didn't get better. There would be no new heart for my Rich.

I don't remember driving home from Philadelphia. I do remember walking into a house that echoed with emptiness. My daughter had left for college just a week earlier. A month before, knowing I would need to be with Rich during his frequent hospitalizations, I'd reluctantly found a good home for my beloved dog. Four months before that, my elderly cat had been put to sleep. Now I was completely alone.

For two weeks I was kept busy with the work and details that come with someone's death. And suddenly that safety net of busyness was all over. I went back to my job as a geriatric nurse, and every evening I came home to an empty house.

I missed Rich dreadfully. I missed sitting on the sofa holding hands. I missed holding him at night. And I especially missed cooking with him. Most evenings, we'd made supper together, each of us leaning against the counters of my old-fashioned kitchen, our hips sometimes bumping while we chopped, diced, simmered, or stirred. Every so often, he would reach down and pat my bottom and tell me that he loved me.

As time passed, instead of feeling better, I found that I was turning inward, happier in my memories than in the real world.

"You need a cat," my sister said.

"You need a cat," my daughter said.

"You need a cat," my friend from work said, "and there's a new litter of kittens at my daughter's farm."

I gave in and visited the farm. There were several yellow tiger-striped kittens running around the living room. When I came in and sat on the sofa, they scattered—all but one. That one ran across the room, bounded onto my lap, and started to nuzzle my cheek.

"I guess I've been chosen," I laughed. I think it was the first time I'd laughed since Rich's death.

My daughter, whose favorite rock band at the time was Mötley Crüe, wanted to name the new family member. That's how I started coming home to a Mötley greeting every night.

Mötley grew into a long, sleek, purring companion who followed me everywhere. He was playful and intelligent, letting me know whenever his food dish was empty and patiently escorting me to the cupboard where the cat food was stored. He curled up at the foot of my bed at night and in my lap while I read. He'd sit on the windows and chitter at the birds nesting under my porch roof. And when Ashley, a long-haired gray puffball, joined our family, Mötley accepted her as though she were his littermate.

One summer evening as I was fixing supper—chopping, dicing, simmering, and stirring—I felt a familiar pat on my bottom. Startled, I automatically turned, half expecting to see Rich. Instead I looked down and saw Mötley. He was sitting on a chair near the kitchen counter, one paw still suspended in the air. He had given me the pat! That yellow tabby stared at me with such love and devotion . . . and then he jumped up to the windowsill and started chittering at a bird outside.

I went back to fixing supper and wondered if someone had taught my Mötley a trick—someone who didn't want me to forget. That was many years ago. Mötley's gone now. So is his companion, Ashley. But today my home includes Murray, Husker, and Miss Kitty. It's Murray who delivers the pats now, to my cheek, my arm, and sometimes to my bottom. It seems that someone still doesn't want me to forget.

As if I ever will.

George and Gracie

By Suzanne Thomas Lawlor

Gracie is known in my home as "The Best Kitty in the World." She is one half of a pair of cats that happily ruled my house in tandem for many years. Her brother, George (also known as "Gorgeous George"), passed on not long ago and now permanently rests in his favorite sunny spot in the garden.

Gracie came into my life first. When my friend's cat had kittens, I asked my husband if we could have a cat. "You can have a cat or a baby," he told me.

I was indignant. "I can have both," I said.

But his comment turned out to be prophetic. When we broke up ten years later, we were childless; he got to stay in the house, and George and Gracie came with me.

It had taken me very little time to pick out my wonderful kitty. She was a tiny mound of gray-striped fur, nursing at the bottom of the furry heap, part of a contented feline clan. I lifted her up and held her to my cheek. When she nuzzled against me, I was a goner. George, however, joined the family a different way. It happened that a couple of weeks after I brought Gracie home, my husband and I went on a long-planned two-week vacation to the Grand Tetons. I was worried about leaving her alone, but she was just getting used to being in our house, and I didn't want to disrupt her new routine. So I asked two of my friends who had cats of their own if they would take turns feeding Gracie and also spend time playing with her. But even with some company every day, Gracie was lonely. Whenever anyone came to the house to feed her, Gracie wailed and made it clear that she was *not* happy.

Being adept problem solvers, my cat sitters hatched a plan. They decided they would get one of Gracie's siblings from the litter as a "loaner kitten." They visited my friend who had the kittens and picked out a little orange and white tabby, the one they thought was the cutest of the litter, and brought him home to Gracie. If he was going to be Gracie's companion, they decided this kitten must be called George (after comedians George Burns and Gracie Allen). When we got back from our trip and saw them curled up in the chair together, there was no turning back.

George let Gracie be the brains of their twenty-year collaboration. But he made up for what he lacked in intelligence with a loving nature. His responsibility was to occupy laps, purr, blink, and be so handsome and endearing that humans would dispense cat treats far beyond the daily ration. Gracie's job was to make all the decisions, do the greetings, remind humans of food and door-opening needs, keep both their coats immaculately clean, and curl up so tightly with George that they became a yin/yang of warm fur that could endure even the coldest Iowa winters. That is, until I moved them to sunny California.

When I left Iowa to return to my hometown in the Bay Area, George and Gracie adapted easily. This was when Gracie took on her most important job around the house: keeping tabs on the emotional needs of all the human occupants and guests. Since then, she's been on call to give comfort, endure tears and periodic bouts of neediness and fervent hugging, and dispense kisses on fingers and faces. Gracie's role as nurturer has been especially appreciated by my parents as they have aged. She is the one that I find lying on my elderly father's shoulder, both of them asleep in the overstuffed chair. And once, when my stepmother, Joan, was so weak at our Christmas dinner that she had to lie down in the bedroom, Gracie got up on the bed with her, to keep her company while the rest of us were finishing our meal. Gracie is a cat you can count on, and she carries out her duties with great diligence.

This was most clear when our beloved George started declining. George was always a heat-seeking cat who loved nothing more than sunbathing. It was his addiction. The only problem was that he had a pure pink nose, and, unfortunately, I wasn't aware that it needed to be protected from the sun. Once he reached fourteen, he developed a spot on his nose that didn't go away. It was skin cancer. For the next four years, I took him periodically to the vet, who would burn off the malignant spot to keep the cancer in check.

When I'd arrive home from the animal hospital and let the half-drugged George out of his kitty carrier, Gracie never failed to greet him. Together they would curl up on the bed while she soothed him with her tender grooming. Seeing the love that Gracie ministered to her Georgie, how they never fought and always stuck close together—either sitting side by side or curled up in a heap of fur—was enough to melt any heart.

Then, George's kidneys started failing, and we knew that his time with us was coming to a close. Each day I thanked him for all he had given me. At night he would crawl under the covers, a new behavior for him, and purr through the night as if to let me know he understood. George ate little now, and, reluctant to leave his side, Gracie adjusted her eating habits, too. We moved the food bowl to the bedroom, but I still worried that neither one was eating enough.

One morning, George, who I knew hadn't eaten for days, emerged from under the bedcovers and his legs gave out. He couldn't move and seemed to be in pain.

This is it, flashed in my brain. I called my vet. After I made the arrangements for her to come to the house to put him to sleep, I carried George out into the garden. I was amazed—he managed to walk, if a bit shakily, to his favorite spot, where the sun shone brightest and longest through the day.

Soon it was time to bring him back inside. I placed him on the bed, and Gracie, who had been escorting him, leapt up to join him. They sat facing the bedroom door on their heating pad, Gracie tightly against him, George with his eyes closed, breathing shallowly. I put my face in his fur, saying my good-byes.

The vet arrived, and I escorted her to the bedroom. The moment she walked into the room, it was as if both cats knew. They immediately turned around with their backs to her. They settled in, with Gracie lying across George. The vet waited until our farewells were over.

I was surprised he went so quickly. As I sensed him leaving, I fell apart. Tossed up by a wave of grief, I exploded into the kind of dry sobs that leave one gasping for breath and coming up empty. I couldn't stop.

Normally Gracie would have come to me. Not now. George was her priority. She continued licking him over and over, and would continue to for the next hour or so. When I picked George up, his body was warm from the heating pad and wet from her ministrations. I wrapped him in a piece of white silk and took his body out into the garden, where I dug a hole in his special sunning spot. I performed a ceremony and placed a large, white, heart-shaped stone, found on other travels, to mark the spot of my beloved companion's resting place.

For months after George's passing, Gracie would often wail for no apparent reason. Even when I went to her, she kept up her crying. Sometimes during the day, but most often at night, this normally quiet cat would walk the hallways of the house, calling out in a strident voice, as though trying to summon George back to her side.

It's been a year now since George left us. Gracie turns twenty-one on June 2. My vet tells me she looks like she is still a kitten. She certainly has a beauty secret I don't have. At night, my little gray-striped cat snuggles near my head—something that only George had done. And so we've settled into our routine without our handsome man about the house.

Some days Gracie's breathing gets wheezy. Always delicate, she now seems fragile. I know the time will come when the vet's medicines, my sister's homeopathy, and all my prayers won't be enough to keep my beloved Gracie with me. I know "The Best Kitty in the World" is destined to join George on the Rainbow Bridge, to greet him with all those tender kisses. In the meantime, I remind Gracie that her work here isn't done. Heaven knows, with all of our trouble getting along with each other, we humans haven't got it right yet. This sweet cat is my reminder to try a little tenderness.

Everyone needs a
friend to lean on.

All cats are born with blue eyes,
but not that many keep them.

Littermates attempting a feline pyramid.

Even a fastidious cat needs a
bath now and then, not that
any cat would ever agree.

The instincts of the hunter never leave even the most domesticated of cats.

Grass: It's good for stalking, eating, and posing in.

Please leave me a message...I seem to be tied up at the moment.

A gray cat is really a black one
with a gene to "dilute"—or
mute—the full expression of color.

Prayers for BB

By Susan Farr-Fahncke

At two-thirty in the morning I awoke to find my eight-year-old, Noah, in tears at my bedside. "I miss BB," he signed to me.

Noah is deaf, and BB, a sweet little gray cat, is his best friend. In the four years we'd had BB, she'd never missed a night of sleeping snuggled up next to him. But three weeks ago, BB had disappeared, only a few days after we'd moved to our new home in Kansas. My heart ached for Noah, as only a mother's can when her child is hurting.

When we'd realized that BB had somehow gotten out of the house, we had begun to search for her right away. We combed the neighborhood and hung up sign after sign, offering a reward. We placed an ad in our city paper, and the kids rode bikes patrolling for her. Still no BB. She had just vanished.

As the days wore on, it became evident that BB was not coming home. A few phone calls in response to our ad brought only disappointment. Deep down, I felt that we would never see her again but couldn't bear to tell Noah. He seemed so lost and lonely without his faithful friend by his side.

Now, I gathered Noah into my arms and prayed with him as we did each night for God to watch over BB and send her back to us. After tucking Noah back into bed, I felt restless and unable to sleep, my heart aching to see my little blue-eyed boy so sad. Noah is sometimes lonely because of his deafness and had been especially so since the move to Kansas. In his silent world, BB's softness, gentle spirit, and constant company had always been a comfort to him.

And so I continued my vigil. Many nights, after Noah was asleep, I'd go to the porch and call to BB, still holding a tiny spark of hope that she would come running across the lawn. Then I'd turn to God again. I'd tell Him that Noah had already experienced great loss in his life. Noah had lost close family members and gone through more sadness than any little boy should. I didn't feel he needed any more "life lessons" right now.

A month went by and still no BB. Whenever we passed the "lost cat" poster for BB on our corner, I saw Noah's face cloud as he was reminded of this latest loss. His loneliness for his little friend was almost too much for me to bear.

Two months passed—an impossibly long time when an animal is missing. I learned that coyotes lived in the woods near our house and realized that they had probably been the fate of our little gray cat. I knew if BB could, she'd have come back to Noah because she adored him. I finally admitted to myself that BB must be dead. Still, I continued to pray.

Then one day my twelve-year-old daughter, Maya, arrived home from school so excited she could barely get the words out. "You need to take me to my friend's house! I think she found BB!"

Maya explained that she had overheard a friend telling some other kids that a gray cat had recently shown up in her yard. She had fed her, so now the cat was hanging around her house.

Maya was almost in tears she was so excited. I was more cautious; I didn't want any more disappointment, for either of us. "Oh, honey, it's hard to believe BB could still be around," I said. "I'll take you there, but don't say anything to Noah."

Leaving the boys with their dad, the girls and I headed off to Maya's friend's house. As we drove across the highway and then a long way into the countryside, I thought to myself that there was no way BB could have gotten this far.

We pulled into the driveway, and Maya's friend came out to meet us, holding a pet carrier. We opened it, and a soft bundle of gray fur tumbled into my arms. I held her up. She did look like BB—right down to those green eyes! Then I immediately felt a jolt of sadness: she didn't have the small white "bikini top" spots that BB had on her chest. I shifted her in my hands, and there they were! Right where my thumbs had been.

"Oh, it's really you! BB! It's you, it's you, it's you!" BB meowed her unique, loud "Rowrrr" at me, and the tears fell as I held our kitty close.

"It's BB!" I told the girls.

Maya giggled and said, "Yeah, we got that."

With shaking hands, I loaded BB into the car. "It's just a miracle!" I told the girls. Minutes later we pulled into the driveway and practically floated through the front door with our little gray bundle in my arms.

The look on Noah's face was the sweetest and most joyful one

I have ever seen. He blinked back tears and signed, "Oh, BB!" He gathered her into his arms and just beamed.

"Whew!" he signed. I knew exactly how he felt.

That night we said some serious "thank-you" prayers, rejoicing that not only had God brought this little miracle back to us, he had completely protected her for two months. She was as soft and healthy as she had been the day she left.

I look at her now, curled up next to Noah, and I wonder where she might have been and what had happened. But I know that she was in God's arms. I believe he heard our prayers and answered them because he knows our hearts and cares deeply about what matters to us. And what mattered to Noah was a special cat who brought joy and comfort to his silent world.

Healing Each Other

By Jeanna Godfrey, D.V.M.

Ben was one of my favorite veterinary clients. A retired cavalry officer who had served in both World Wars, he was the epitome of an officer and a gentleman. Over the years, I had treated his horses, and we had become good friends. In retirement, Ben had three passionate loves—his wife of over fifty years, Mary, a feisty Arabian gelding named Geronimo, and a three-legged cat named Tripod.

The story of Ben and Tripod began one spring morning when Ben was in picking up some supplements for Geronimo and asking me about vaccination schedules. I could tell something was troubling him. He seemed preoccupied, and his usual smiling face was pinched and drawn. I had finished my morning surgeries, so I invited Ben to have a cup of coffee and escorted him into my office. I was just about to ask if anything was wrong when my receptionist came in.

"Dr. Godfrey, sorry to interrupt, but there's a lady on the phone who says she just found a cat in her back yard with a badly hurt leg."

"I'll take it," I said, smiling ruefully at Ben. I handed him his coffee and picked up the phone on my desk. "This is Dr. Godfrey. How can I help you?"

"Doctor, I apologize for calling, but I don't know what to do!" The women's voice was almost frantic. "There's a big tom cat lying outside my back door. His front leg is all mangled and bloody and just hanging there! The poor thing looks terrible, but I'm not really a cat person, and I'm afraid to try to pick him up."

"Do you have any idea who owns him?" I asked. "Can you see any collar or tag on him?"

"I did get close enough to check, but there's no collar." The woman was close to tears. "I really think he must be a stray. He's not been neutered, and he has some old scars on his head. The poor thing. . . ."

I assured the kindhearted woman that I was happy to help and wrote down the address of her home, just a few minutes away. "I have two pre-vet students in the clinic today. I'll send them right out to pick up the cat." I also asked the woman if she'd mind checking around the neighborhood to see if she could locate an owner.

I turned back to Ben as I hung up the phone. "Can you a wait a minute, Ben? This is an emergency."

I went up front and explained the situation to the students. "If the cat's wild, you may not be able to get close to him, but we can at least try." They eagerly accepted the challenge and ran to the truck.

I returned to my office in the hopes of finding out what was troubling my friend. I settled back in my chair and picked up my coffee. I saw that Ben had hardly touched his.

"Ben, I don't mean to pry, but you're not yourself today. Is something wrong?"

Several seconds went by before he answered.

"Well, I just came from the doctor, and it appears I have cancer," my old friend said faintly.

I sat quietly as Ben told me of the symptoms he'd had, the tests that had been run, and the results he'd been given less than an hour before. We discussed his treatment options, and I was offering some words of comfort when I heard the students returning with my latest patient.

"Ben, I've got to tend to this cat," I said, getting up from my desk. "Please stay and finish your coffee." I hesitated at the office door. "Unless you'd like to come and help?" Having survived two World Wars, Ben probably knew as much about wound care as I did, and I thought this might take his mind off his troubles.

"Yes, I'd like to see the poor fellow." Ben was quick to put his own worries aside when there was an animal in need. We reached the treatment area just as the students sat the carrier down.

"Boy, Dr. G. We had to drive with the windows down, the smell from that leg is so bad. This guy's in pretty poor shape."

I gently removed the large gray tabby from the cat carrier and placed him on the exam table. He lay very still, his breathing rapid and shallow. His right front leg was mutilated from just below the shoulder. The students hadn't exaggerated; the odor coming from the rotting flesh was overpowering.

"Looks like he was caught in a trap. See those ragged wound edges?" I felt the ice-cold toes and footpads, recognizing there was little chance, if any, of saving the leg. Ben and the students hovered around the treatment table as I completed my initial exam.

"I wish we knew if he had an owner," I murmured, gently

inserting a catheter into the vein on his good leg. "The only way I can save him is to amputate that leg, but he'd have to be an inside cat afterward with someone able to give him lots of care. And even with surgery his chances are pretty slim."

I started warmed fluids running into his vein to counteract shock and dehydration and administered a large dose of antibiotics. My audience watched in somber silence as I carefully cleaned the wound. I knew from years of experience that this little guy probably didn't have an owner. My suspicion was confirmed when my receptionist stuck her head into the treatment area.

"The lady called back. She's spoken with her neighbors. Several said they'd seen the cat roaming in the area over the last few months, but he doesn't appear to have an owner. At least not one who cares about him."

"Well, then," I sighed, "it's either remove the leg and see if we can find a home for him, or put him to sleep." Just at that moment, Ben began stroking the cat's head. Somewhere deep in the tom's throat, a faint purr began, and as Ben continued to pet the tabby, I noticed the cat's breathing became less labored.

"You're a fighter, aren't you, boy?" Ben whispered softly as he rubbed the cat's head. "You deserve a chance, don't you, good fella?" Ben looked up at me, and I knew in that instant I'd do everything in my power to save this poor kitty. Somehow his fate and that of my dear friend seemed inexplicably bound together.

I performed the operation the next morning. Ben had returned for the surgery, anxiously waiting in the reception area. When I was done and the patient was as stable as possible, I came out to join Ben.

"Well, Ben, I can't make any guarantees, but he made it through the amputation, and his vital signs are okay right now." I sat down next to the old gentlemen. "The main thing we have to worry about is infection. That could still do him in."

"I know you did everything you could, Jeanna." He patted my hand as he spoke. "I guess it's up to him and the good Lord now."

Over the next few weeks, Tripod (I had allowed the students who rescued him to provide a name) went through many ups and downs—as did Ben. His chemotherapy was started almost immediately, and although that slowed him down, he came by the clinic as frequently as he could. We would help him into a chair in the treatment area and bring Tripod to lie on his lap. Ben would stroke the young cat and tell him what a strong and handsome boy he was while Tripod lay very still, purring contentedly.

These sessions continued for several weeks. I was cautiously optimistic about Tripod's recovery. It had taken extensive antibiotic therapy and lots of nursing care to overcome the infection, but the cat still had a way to go, so I hesitated to give Ben a favorable prognosis.

One morning Ben came by for his usual "therapy session with Tripod" as he jokingly referred to their time together.

"I won't be able to visit him for a week or so," he said, rubbing the spot along Tripod's chin that always elicited an especially appreciative purr. "I have to go to Houston for some tests . . . to see if the chemo worked."

The next two weeks were busy at the practice, but every chance I got, I would sneak Tripod into my office, place him gently on my lap, and do my best to cuddle and stroke him as Ben had done. Tripod was definitely out of danger now and each day became stronger and more adept at moving around on three legs. Then one morning, Ben was back. I only had to look at the smile on his face to know the news had been good. I got up from my desk and gave him a big hug.

"How's my boy?" he said, the smile momentarily gone in anticipation of bad news.

"Well, I guess you'd better see for yourself." I smiled as I opened the door, knowing full well Tripod would be sitting outside, awaiting our morning "therapy session."

Ben's eyes grew wide as Tripod loped into the office. His body was still thin, but his eyes were bright, and his coat had the shine of good health. Without hesitating, the slim cat jumped effortlessly into Ben's lap and arranged himself for some serious petting.

Ben gently stroked Tripod's chin, then broke into a big smile. I heard him whisper, "We made it together, didn't we, boy?"

And to this day, I swear that cat smiled back.

Morning Coffee

By Jack Frye

A s I sit here looking eastward at the new sunrise, my coffee-drinking buddies, Strike and George, come to mind. George was a long-haired solid-orange cat, and Strike was a short-haired white cat with black markings on his ears and tail. Strike also had three black spots on his side in the form of a triangle, just like the holes in a bowling ball—and so his name.

Every morning for years, the three of us would make our way to the backyard and sit on the swing or position ourselves along the fence—me leaning against it, George and Strike balancing gracefully on top of it—and get ready for the show. The coffee would warm my hands, and their presence would warm my heart.

Mornings were the special times when the cats and I could just enjoy the peace and quiet, before daylight showed us the reality of our world. There is something about the hush just before the sun starts peeking over the horizon that makes one want to listen to the silence. That may sound odd, but it's just what we did.

Some mornings as we walked out to our viewing spot, there would be frost on the ground so that each of my steps would make a crunching sound. At times the sound was so loud in the stillness that I'd try to tiptoe, afraid that I would wake the sleeping birds and start their songs too early. Once we got to the spot, I'd look back toward the house and see my footprints with their little paw prints right beside them showing the trail we had made. As we waited for the dawn, I would pick out the stars that I knew and guess at what colors the sunrise would be. Then, at the first hint of the sun, the cat's ears would perk up, swiveling toward the sounds starting to emerge all around us. The birds would begin their singing—at first, as soft as a gentle whisper, calling out on the breeze, then soaring, their songs filling the morning air with life. There were times when I felt we were listening to a concert written just for the three of us. The birds always had a way of lifting our spirits high, as if they knew the hardships we would face once the rest of the world woke up.

As the first rays of sunlight appeared, glowing with a reddish tint, they highlighted the trees off in the distance. The breeze moving through the branches made them look as if they were stretching in order to wake up. The higher the sun rose, the more the birds flew around, searching for their morning meal. It was about then that the neighborhood dogs, hungry for their breakfast and ready to begin their daily routines, would start to bark, disturbing the birds' concert.

But we didn't mind. By this time, the show was over, the light of day once again filling the everyday landscape. As we headed into the house, I'd glance back over my shoulder and marvel at just how much hope there was in a sunrise. I'd say a little prayer of thankfulness and ask for strength to care for our loved one inside. My wife had Huntington's disease, a neurological disorder, and we were her team, George and Strike giving her the healing balm of purrs, rubs, and head butts, while I gave her the medicines from the doctors.

The cats asked for so little and gave my wife and me so much. They seemed to know that I needed someone to sit beside me and listen, and that she needed someone to sit in her lap and shower love on her, especially as her illness progressed. It meant a lot to me that, although they could come and go as they pleased, they still chose to spend those mornings with me and the rest of the day with her. They got us through a very rough time.

I will always remember the way they brought a smile to her face in her last days. The cats seemed to understand that because of the Huntington's disease she could no longer control the movements of her body, and they often responded to them. The three of them moving together in her chair appeared to be dancing—bebopping to a song that only they could hear. Strike and George kept a sparkle in her eyes that shone on them like the rays of the sun we had witnessed rising earlier.

The day she left the house for the last time, the cats sat for hours in the open doorway she had gone through. I couldn't bring myself to move them and close the door. Each time I walked by, they'd look up at me with sadness in their eyes and then turn to stare back out the door. I'd pat and stroke them, but I couldn't get a purr out of them. I put their water and food bowls beside them, but they didn't eat or drink all day. When the sun went down that evening, they finally let me shut the door.

The next morning they walked to the backyard with me once again for our morning coffee. The three of us spent a lot of time together out there in the following weeks and months. They never seemed to tire of my stories and always knew when to purr and rub against me to cheer me up. Today those two cats are more than just a memory to me. Thinking of them, I still feel a bond with them—a bond so close that I know they'll always be a part of who I am. They showed me how much it means to stand by the people you love. George and Strike weren't just cats; they were also teachers, companions, caregivers, and friends. But most of all, they were family.

Molly's Baby

By Mary Lynne Hill

After the death of our cat, my husband and I, deeply saddened, decided "no more pets." Not a cat, a dog, a fish, or an ostrich. No pets. It was too hard to lose them. But we make plans, and the gods? Well, the gods—they laugh at us. This time, the gods' laughter came in the form of a young, long-haired calico cat waiting for me at our front door one day.

My husband and I had finished graduate school and recently moved to a cabin in the Texas Hill Country. The cat was sitting there as if she had been expecting me, looking up at me as if she wanted to know why I was late. I unlocked the front door and *zip!*—in she went, planting herself in the middle of the living room floor. As I politely scooted her out the door, she looked at me in confusion, clearly wondering why she was being put out in the yard. I naively thought, *Well, that's that,* and closed the door firmly.

Later that evening, my husband came home, opened the front door, and *zip!* There she was again, planting her furry self in the middle of the living room as if she belonged there. This time, my husband scooted her out the door and closed it firmly. After several days of zipping and scooting, we gave in. We had posted signs throughout our neighborhood to see if anyone had lost her but had received no calls. So we let down our guard and welcomed her into our home. We had been adopted.

We didn't have any children, so before long, the cat we called Molly was rather spoiled. But as we got to know Molly, we realized that she was also quite maternal. This temperament revealed itself most obviously in her nightly routine of putting "her babies," our name for her toy mice, to bed. Each evening, she would gather up each of her babies, one by one, and place them all together in one of various locations she deemed secure. As she carried each one to that night's sleeping spot, she emitted a distinctive, deep, and guttural purr. This was the only time she ever used that particular purr. After she had placed them all in the safe space, say, under the corner of our bed, she would lie with them for a few minutes, completing her tuck-in process. Once she was assured that they were "asleep," she would patrol the house, checking doors, windows, and people before settling down herself. She maintained this routine every night for many years.

Then one January evening, two blue lines showed up on my pregnancy test. We were overjoyed. Molly seemed to know I was pregnant and immediately decided it was her job to protect me. For the next nine months, she watched me like a hawk, but still took time out each night to gather her babies and tuck them in with that satisfied purr.

Around 3:00 AM, on September 17, 2005, my very pregnant body woke me up to let me know that something was definitely moving and shaking. I ponderously hoisted myself up and sat on the edge of the bed. Looking down, I saw Molly's deep green eyes boring into me. She was watching me with such intensity that it started to creep me out.

I got up, trying not to disturb my husband, who was sleeping soundly. Molly was slithering around my swollen ankles like some possessed creature from an Alfred Hitchcock thriller. After a few minutes, I decided that, yes, things were shifting and changing in my body, but I was fine. So I climbed back into bed. As I closed my eyes to drift into a rough sleep, the last thing I saw were Molly's enormous eyes two inches from mine; I could feel her breath warm upon my face.

This was weird behavior for Molly, who never slept near our heads. She would occasionally sleep at the foot of our bed, but generally she slept in her own spaces with her babies. But now as my body shifted into labor mode, I became the tree and Molly the summer leaves covering me. For the rest of the night, when I rolled over in bed, she climbed to the other side of me, so she could continue to monitor my breathing. When I finally got up and showered, she sat outside the shower—though she usually hated being in the "splash zone"—so she could make sure I didn't fall. Later, when I waddled over to lie down on the couch and watch TV, she padded after me, so she could spoon her body around the unborn baby's to protect it. She was in heightened-protection maternal mode, and I found myself trying not to cry when I had to leave her to go to the hospital. I was pretty sure that the medical personnel would frown upon me showing up with an overly anxious cat at Labor and Delivery.

The birth went well. Ten fingers, ten toes, and a set of lungs that matched our son's ten-pound, two-ounce, twenty-one-inch body. Whiskers twitching, Molly's face loomed large in the window next to the front door as we brought A.J. up the sidewalk for the first time. We carried him into the house and settled in for our new life. Molly circled around us, meowing incessantly, chastising us for how rude we had been to leave her at home when clearly she had been needed at the hospital.

I had been warned about babies and cats and wondered if I had to protect A.J. from our furry family member. Molly, sensing my uncertainty, played it wisely: though clearly interested, she always maintained a discreet distance. Over the next few weeks, she carefully placed herself at the edge of our bed, where she could still peer into the bassinet. If someone were sitting on the couch holding the baby, Molly would climb onto the back of the couch, so she could see over the holder's shoulder. If I put A.J. on a blanket, Molly would curl up on the edge of it, occasionally sniffing him, but not lying so close that she could accidentally roll over onto him. However, she was never so far away from A.J. that she wouldn't be the first line of defense against anything or anyone who might harm him.

My body throbbing with exhaustion one evening, I checked the sleeping baby in the bassinette next to me one more time. Then I fell into bed and pulled the covers up under my chin. Molly had climbed onto our bed so she, too, could peer into the bassinette one more time. Satisfied that the baby's breath was regular, and he was sleeping soundly, she snuggled down into the covers against my feet. As she did this, I turned to my husband, who was looking at me with a surprised expression on his face that matched my own. We had both suddenly realized that since we'd brought A.J. home from the hospital, we had not once heard the deep guttural purr of Molly putting her babies to bed in the evening.

Molly's nightly routine had changed, now that she had a real baby of her very own to look after.

Just Do It

By B. J. Taylor

I stood in the veterinarian's office that warm August day waiting for the test results with my marmalade-colored cat, Red. The vet had been concerned at our last visit because Red, always a "big boy," had lost a considerable amount of weight within the span of a few months. On top of that, his coat was no longer shiny, and his hind legs wobbled when he walked.

The vet entered the room. "The tests confirm it. He has diabetes," he said kindly as he stroked Red's head. He went on to tell me it was very common in cats, but it could be managed and he could live a full life. This didn't sound too bad—until I asked him what the treatment would be.

"You'll have to feed him special diabetic-formula cat food, and you'll need to give him an insulin shot twice a day."

A shot! Just the thought of a needle made my heart race with fear. I barely heard the vet as he wrote out a prescription for the insulin and described the syringes and brand of cat food I'd need to buy. I wasn't afraid of the cost of the supplies to keep Red healthy. I would buy anything my furry friend needed. But give him a shot with a needle? I just didn't know if I could.

In the car on the ride home, I stuck my finger through one of the slots on the cat carrier and stroked Red's head. He was ten years old, but it seemed like a short time ago that I had first laid eyes on him. "Marmalade kitten found in alley. Home needed," the handwritten sign proclaimed in the storefront window. I'd always wanted an orange and white kitty, but I had three cats already. *What's one more?* I thought. I called the number and a young woman brought him right over. She held the meowing kitten tightly against her chest as she got out of the car. "Will you take good care of him?"

"I will. I promise," I said, as I reached for the squirming bundle of fur. Red settled in, and things had gone well, until he lost all that weight.

I got home and brought Red's carrier into the house. He stepped out and wobbled to the water dish. I pulled the prescriptions out of my purse, plopped down on the couch, and closed my eyes. Clammy fear spread through my body as I remembered that horrible day in the hospital many years ago when I was in for some outpatient surgery. A nurse's aide entered the room with a cheery attitude and a silver steel tray. "I'm here to start your IV," she said breezily. She put the rubber hose around my upper arm, turned my palm face up, and then poked me once to find a vein. Then she poked me again. And again. And again. "I can't seem to find a vein," she said. "Yours are very small. Let me call someone else to try." Her supervisor entered the room, and she tried three times. Then another nurse came in, turned my arm over, and found a vein in the top of my hand.

"That hurt," I said to the three of them crowded around my bedside.

"Sorry, that's the best we can do." They slapped tape across the needle and pressed down hard. By this time, my hand and arm were throbbing. I wanted to cry.

Years later I went for a blood draw for some tests. I turned my face to the wall and tried to remain calm by thinking of a favorite vacation spot, a hot fudge sundae, anything to keep my mind off what she was about to do. I felt the needle inserted once, then twice.

"Owwww!" I couldn't help but cry out. I knew I shouldn't be a baby—others go through this and so much worse—all the time. But each time I've had to face a needle in the many years since then, I break out in a cold sweat, my hands become clammy, and my heart races like a jackhammer.

Now I had to give my beloved cat a shot—twice a day. I purchased all the supplies, then drove to the vet's office with Red. "Show me how to do it," I said. He filled a syringe with sugar water. "You pinch his fur on the back of his neck, insert the needle quickly, and then press the plunger. Here, you try."

My hands shook as I filled the needle to the required dosage. "I don't think I can do this."

"Sure you can," he said. "And it will get easier."

I took the needle and did as he instructed. Oh, how I hated the thought of doing this twice a day, but the vet assured me Red would get better. Even his back legs, which were wobbly from nerve damage, would straighten up after he was on the medication for a while.

The next morning, when Red needed his shot, I froze. *How can I do this when I'm feeling so scared?* I took a deep breath and carefully drew the right amount of insulin into the needle. Then I called Red. He walked into the kitchen and stood calmly. I looked at my beloved cat, the one who always jumped up on the couch and snuggled next to me, who looked to me to take care of him and rescue him if need be, just as I had when he was an orphan kitten. *Just do it.* I reached down and pinched a bit of skin, inserted the needle, and pressed the plunger. He never even moved. I rubbed the top of Red's head and stroked his scraggly fur. He sauntered back into the living room, stretched out in a patch of sunlight streaming through the window, and went to sleep.

Slowly, Red began to get better. I still didn't like the needles, but it did get easier, and knowing Red needed the medication kept me going. Then late one day I received a call from my doctor's office. She wanted to schedule me for some necessary surgery. That meant needles and pain. I told the nurse I'd think about it and hung up the phone.

I sank back against the counter, that old clammy fear creeping up my spine. Just then Red walked into the kitchen and rubbed against my legs. I loved having my healthy, head-rubbing cat back. His coat was shiny and full, and his hind legs no longer wobbled. Red trusted me to help him get better and took every shot with ease, standing still for the quick plunge, then lifting his head high and trotting off to his favorite resting spot of the day. He definitely had the right attitude. To him, the shots were no big deal. *Come on,* I told myself, *you can do it, too.* I called the nurse back.

The morning of the surgery, as I lay on the bed in the prep room at the hospital, I kept my mind on the thought of Red lounging in the warmth of the sun pouring through the living room window. I rested my head against the pillow, took a deep breath, and let peace flow through me. It was going to be fine— I could handle this. Thanks to Red, I had faced my fear and let it go.

Nothing escapes the attention of a curious cat.

Few animals look
as contented asleep
as the cat.

A solid gray color is
preferred in some breeds,
but is just gorgeous anyway.

Why are some cats always
drawn to warm, clean laundry?

Cubby holes are perfect for a game of peek-a-boo.

This is one of too many shelter cats who find themselves in need of new homes.

Long-haired cats are beautiful, but even they can have a bad hair day.

A kitten adds happiness to any home.

¡Caliente!

By Marty Becker, D.V.M.

I was catching up on paperwork one summer evening at my southern Idaho veterinary hospital when suddenly I heard a loud pounding on the back door. Startled and a little alarmed, I peeked out the window of the office door. There on the steps was a Hispanic couple and their two children. The mother held a box, and the father carried something bundled in a blanket, but no animal was visible.

Reading the urgency in their body language, I opened the door and was overcome by the smell of smoke and a cacophony of explanations that, with only two years of high school Spanish, I couldn't begin to decipher. The man held the bundle out to me. I lifted the edge of the blanket and saw a badly burned cat lying on her side. The skin on the bottom of her foot pads was hanging in charred strips, much of the fur on her head and neck and all of her whiskers were burned off, and she was squinting from the pain of her burned corneas. I also noticed she had enlarged teats, which gave me a good indication of what was in the box the woman held.

Dehydration being the biggest and most urgent threat to any

burn victim, I motioned for the family to follow me into the treatment room where I put the cat on a heavy towel. With the mother and children on one side of the table whispering nervously to each other, I showed the father how to hold the cat for me, and started an intravenous drip to rehydrate her. While I was examining her, the cat kept making mournful sounds, which at first I took to be cries of pain. But as the sounds intensified, I noticed her focus on the box. Looking inside, I saw six beautiful, black-and-gray tiger-striped kittens with singed fur, but otherwise none the worse for wear. Their eyes still closed from birth, they were meowing for their mother and her milk.

About that time, a fifth family member came knocking on the back door. This high school–aged young man spoke English quite well, and soon I had the whole story. They were a migrant family who had been working the fields, thinning sugar beets, when they noticed that a nearby haystack was on fire. It seems the first cutting of hay had been put up wet, and subsequently the stack caught fire via spontaneous combustion. Clearly, the haystack was going to be lost, so the farm owner, his wife, and the migrant family focused on wetting down neighboring structures with hoses and buckets, so the fire wouldn't spread.

After a frantic and ultimately successful battle to contain the fire, they had stopped to catch their breath when they saw something coming out of the smoke around the haystack. It was a cat with a kitten in its mouth. Following the cat to a small calving shed, they found five other kittens in a sleepy heap. Despite the innate fear of fire all animals share, this determined mother had gone back to her kittens' birthplace, plunging headfirst into the burning stack six times to rescue her kittens. One by one, she had grabbed each of the kittens by the scruff of the neck, taken it to safety, and gone back for the next. The kittens' eyes were still closed, so they weren't damaged, and their feet never touched the burning embers on the ground, so their tiny foot pads were still soft and pink. But Momma cat had paid a tremendous physical price for saving all of her babies.

With the mother cat stabilized, the son made introductions, and I started the medical record, which included names, address, and how they were going to pay, along with information about the pet. The son explained that the injured cat was one of the barn cats on the farm where the family was working. The farmer had made it clear that he didn't want to spend a lot of money on the cat, except in this case, to put her out of her misery. He had given his permission for the family to take the cat and kittens to the vet for medical attention—but it would have to be on their dime.

I had seen this family's old car when I first went to the door. I saw the clothes they wore. Coming from a farm background myself, I knew the plight of migrant families firsthand. I also knew I'd be giving them a discount, a fire sale of sorts, but they didn't. Considering that they didn't have much money, I wondered, why would this family drop everything to take responsibility for a severely injured cat and kittens that they didn't even own.

When I asked the boy, he turned to his parents with the question, and suddenly the room got very quiet. After a moment the man pointed to the woman, who undid the top couple of buttons of her shirt to reveal a badly burned chest. The scars were so severe I winced. The boy explained that his mother, as a young girl, had reached up and grabbed the handle of a pot on the stove, pouring boiling water all down her chest and legs. Through her son, the woman told me she knew how painful burns were and how disfiguring, but she also remembered how her mother had loved her and nursed her back to health. She also took comfort in knowing that her own husband and children adored her as she was. She, and the whole family, were going to do no less for the cat and her kittens.

Moved by their compassion, I went back to filling in the information on the necessary paperwork. When I asked the family if they had a name for the cat, even a temporary one we could put on the chart, they buzzed for a few moments, then looked at me, all smiling broadly. The boy said, "We're going to call her Caliente!"

Mrs. Lagrone, my high school Spanish teacher, would have killed me if I hadn't remembered that that word means "hot." A perfect name for a heroic cat who, with some major medical treatment and lots of TLC, would be restored to health and cherished always by a very special family.

The Cat Who Breathed for Me

By Marcia E. Brown

The winter of 1970 was one of the worst I knew in all my years living in Detroit. By December, hospitals were overflowing with folks suffering from flu and pneumonia. I became one of the epidemic statistics as an upper respiratory infection laid me low just before Christmas.

Holiday cooking and decorating came to a halt. My sons, eleven and thirteen, tried to carry on, as my husband was out of town. But in the midst of it all, Tuffy, our fifteen-pound Maine coon cat, was full of mischief as usual. Tuffy had never been an easy cat to live with. He was half grown when he came to us, and his previous owner had played good-naturedly but roughly with him. As a result, he was sometimes a holy terror with us. He never scratched the children, but with me, it was no-holds-barred, which all too often meant claws out! And he took delight in jumping out at us from around corners and startling us.

The first time he did this, my younger son said, "I think maybe he was too young to leave his mother!"

Perhaps he was. But he also could be the most delightful of cats, and we loved him.

We left small plastic bottles of water around the house, so we could squirt him when he was in his wild pouncing mood. None of us wanted to give him up. When he was good, he was so sweet and lovable that we forgave him when he was the proverbial "horrid." We knew he meant no harm. Really! This was just his idea of fun. Often when I was resting or reading, he would stretch out on my lap and be the picture of purring contentment and affection. Most of the time, he talked, as cats will, rubbed up against us, played nicely, and wormed his feline way into our hearts as a member of the family.

As Christmas approached, my upper respiratory infection suddenly grew worse. Then, one day, I just could not get my breath. Unable to talk and feeling panicky, I scribbled a note to my older son, Dave, telling him to call our doctor and ask if I could be admitted to the hospital, for I could feel my lungs filling. The streets were icy with snow that had packed, frozen, melted, and refrozen, but I thought surely an ambulance could come for me. No such luck!

The doctor told Dave that I must stay home, that all the city's hospitals were so full that people were on cots in the hallways, and there was not enough staff to help everyone. Many doctors and nurses were stranded at home following the latest blizzard. He did promise to try to have a pharmacy deliver medicine to me. Meanwhile, he said, I should remain in bed and rest.

With difficulty, I climbed the stairs to my room, struggling for breath. I got into bed and lay there tensely, frightened by the difficulty I was having breathing and unable to move without feeling my condition worsen. Eventually, the medicine was delivered, but it didn't help right away. I told my boys to keep away, as I didn't want them to get sick, too.

After a while, I caught sight of two ears and then Tuffy's full face looking up from my bedside quizzically, as if trying to decipher what was happening. Then, *pounce!* He landed on the bed, climbed up onto me, and lay down on my chest almost nose to nose with me.

He was heavy! I remember thinking, *He's keeping my chest from rising when I'm so weak. I may just die from a fifteen-pound cat perched on my chest!* But I was too sick to do anything about it.

We were eye to eye, Tuffy's looking deeply into my own, hardly blinking. His breath was warm on my face. His breathing slowed to match mine. Gradually, steadily, I relaxed under his warmth and reached up one hand to stroke his fur. Tuffy stretched his long body until he almost covered mine, and began to purr. There was absolutely no doubt that he was trying his very best to help me. And he did. Somehow I became less anxious, less afraid—less sure I would die—and the medication finally began to take effect.

Later, when I was better, my sons told me that Tuffy stayed with me for three days and nights, leaving only once a day to eat and, I presume, to use his litter box. After those first hours of lying on me as if to share with me his very breath, he had moved over to stretch out at my side and offer his warmth and comfort. Our feisty, yet loving cat knew I needed healing, and that's what he gave.

Furry Family Members

A Hemingway Tale

By Lisa Finch

"Hailey, I don't think she likes that," I said to my ten-year-old daughter. Our sleek black cat, Bella, squirmed in her arms. Bella broke free and pounced from Hailey's embrace, casting a look of disdain at her former captor. Hailey sighed and walked to her room with a decided slump in her shoulders. "Why won't Bella ever let me snuggle with her?"

"That's just not how most cats are," I explained. "You want a cat that acts like a dog."

Hailey definitely needed an animal she could cuddle with. I paid a visit to our local Society for the Prevention of Cruelty to Animals (SPCA) in search of a small dog, but unfortunately, none were to be had that day. On my way out, I walked through the lobby of the shelter and couldn't help noticing the two large, glass-enclosed cases dominating the room. In the left one, two adorable kittens pawed the glass. "Pick me! Love me!" they seemed to say. They would find homes in no time. To the right, far back in the enclosure, a sad-eyed, fluffy orange cat looked over at me. The sign on the glass above him said "trapped."

"What's his story?" I asked the SPCA staff member.

"Oh him! He's got personality plus," she said, joining me by the glass.

I looked closer. Sitting far back in the cage, paws tucked in, scowling, he didn't appear very personable. In fact, he seemed downright despondent. Well, who wouldn't be, locked in a glass case?

The key was slipped into the lock, and an immediate transformation took place. Orange cat sprang to life and ran to us, purring and meowing loudly. He nuzzled up to me, pushing his face into my leg. "Wow, he really does have personality plus," I said. "He was trapped?"

She nodded. "Someone in the neighborhood here traps every animal that steps foot on his property. We brought this little guy in three weeks ago. He's been fixed, and he's got a collar, but it had no identifying information." She leaned down to pet him with me. "He was somebody's pet for sure."

"And no one came to claim him?"

She shook her head. I couldn't believe it. Three weeks, and no one showed up for him. "What's he like with other cats?" I pictured Bella less than amused if I brought this little fellow home.

"I don't know. Let's see," she said. We took Mr. Orange and the "pick me" kittens into an adjoining room. The kittens jumped and frolicked; Mr. Orange allowed them to walk all over him, literally. He hardly glanced in their direction.

"He's polydactyl," the lady said. "See? Six toes." She picked up his front paws and showed me his extra digit. His paws looked like catcher's mitts.

"They say that Hemingway raised polydactyl cats," she went on to explain.

Hemingway. I stroked his beautiful long-haired coat, and he flipped over on his back, paws in the air. I'd never really known a cat who demanded so much attention and affection. I spoke with the lady a while longer, saying that I might be back and that I was definitely interested.

I left the building feeling like I'd left part of myself behind. But there was still one person I needed to convince before I committed to adopting Hemingway. I called my husband, Chris, and told him there was someone I needed him to meet.

"Who?"

"It's a little friend at the SPCA," I said, cringing. We already had a cat, fish, and a hamster. He'd made it plain that he thought we had more than enough pets.

He sighed. "Just go get it then," he said, sounding defeated.

"No, I want you to meet him first. He's a very sweet orange cat. His name is Hemingway."

"Hemingway? That's his name?"

"Well, that's what I call him. . . ."

"You named him!" He groaned.

We agreed to meet back at the SPCA. Chris beat me there by several minutes. When I walked in, Chris was seated in a chair, filling out the adoption papers, Hemingway spread across his lap. I had to laugh.

He looked up at me and grinned sheepishly. "Okay, you're right," he said. "We have to take this guy home."

Our kids would be thrilled. Two days later, I brought Hemingway home. The kids knew that after school, they'd meet their new pet. Chris was at work. Hemingway would have the day to adjust to his new surroundings and his potential playmate, Bella.

It didn't take him long to relax and leave the safe haven of the laundry room, where a new litter box, a dish of dry food, and a bowl of fresh water had been set out for him. He ventured, slowly, into the family room and then upstairs. Hemingway peered down the hallway. Bella, emerging from my bedroom, stopped in her tracks. They exchanged a few warning hisses and stayed out of each other's way. *Could be worse,* I thought.

Hemingway stayed by my side while Bella ran for cover under my bed. I got down on my knees and took a good look at our new cat. His beautiful golden eyes looked into mine. I scratched his head. Now I'd have a chance to really get to know him. He put both paws up on my shoulders, as if in an embrace, and got right into my face. I'd never known a cat to get so up close and personal this quickly. *Would he bite me?* I didn't really know him, after all. He kissed my face.

"Where did you come from, Hemingway? And how is it that no one came to find you?" He purred loudly and continued kissing me. *Somebody's great loss,* I thought, *and our gain.* I felt a little sorry for whoever lost him. But I also thanked my lucky stars that I happened to go into our local SPCA when I did.

Now, how would he survive the next challenge? Little did he know about the three very excited children who would pounce on him after school. I had warned the kids to take it slowly, not to crowd Hemingway. Their eyes had glazed over, and I was sure they hadn't heard a word I said. Sure enough, rushing into the room after school, they held him in their arms and petted him. He purred, rolled over to have his belly rubbed, and kissed their faces. They laughed with delight. This cat was something new in their experience.

Bella seemed to heave a giant sigh of relief and was now free to pursue her own interests without being picked up, petted, or otherwise hounded. Hemingway, on the other hand, ate up the affection with a spoon.

He didn't just like attention. He demanded it. One night our family played a board game, and apparently Hemingway didn't like the idea. He ran to the middle of the board, stole a game token, and ran off. Chris and I exchanged surprised looks. The kids broke into gales of laughter.

"I guess we weren't paying him enough attention," I said and chased after him to retrieve the game piece.

He loved visitors, too. His motto seemed to be that there was enough of him to go around. It wasn't unusual for him to perch across two people at the same time, so they could both pet him. Bella, on the other hand, had always had a disdainful air about "outsiders" and didn't welcome company.

At first, Bella enjoyed being left alone, but then a strange thing happened. She started coming around, more and more, seeking affection. It wasn't the "I'll roll over so you can pet my belly" display that Hemingway was known for, but for Bella, it was a big step. She even ventured out when company visited. "Wow, I don't think I've ever seen her before," people said when Bella appeared.

"Mom!" Hailey yelled out one day. "Bella let me kiss her!"

In a way, we got a two-for-one deal: Hemingway and a more

affectionate Bella. She saw what Hemingway demanded and decided it was a pretty good deal after all—well, in small doses anyway. She still bites Chris when he comes to bed after working nights, but that's only to make it clear who owns the bed. After all, he's just disturbed her beauty rest. It's a simple warning nip— nothing personal.

Hemingway still laps up the attention and meows for more. Fortunately, in our house, there's always enough love to go around.

Leader of the Pack

By Felice Prager

Smokey had always been a shy cat. When his older sister, Bumper, was alive, he did nothing without her. She made the decisions, and like a perfectly content mate, he followed. Bumper was the queen, the boss. She was in charge, so Smokey had no need to be. For the most part, except at night when he cuddled in our bed against my husband's or my legs, Smokey was the cat no one ever saw. He purred loudly and seemed happy and healthy when he was with us, but he never seemed interested in any other role than that of the timid cat who lived under the bed.

If we went away for a few days, on our return, the cat sitters would often comment that there was no sign of Smokey. They seemed to think we were inventing Smokey, but we knew otherwise. Since his food bowl was empty in the morning, and we knew he was the only one of our three cats who preferred canned food, we had evidence that he was alive and well. Sometimes, we actually saw him eating, but this was only when he followed Bumper to their bowls. Outside of his safe haven, Smokey did nothing independently, and we accepted this as his unique personality; he was a sweet cat who was a follower.

We were very worried about Smokey when Bumper got sick and died, because we didn't know if he could cope, or even survive, without her. But eventually Smokey decided to come out from under the bed by himself. I suppose he got hungry, or maybe he just got lonely. Then, a few weeks after Bumper's death, as if it were nothing new, Smokey began coming into our family room in the evenings and curling up in a ball on a blanket near us. Sometimes he even sat on our laps. Our youngest cat, Cleopatra, often jumped up and cuddled with him. Smokey never fussed about this. In fact, he shifted his body to make room for her. It was as if she filled a space that had been empty for him since Bumper had died. When we saw him grooming his younger sister, we took it as a sign that Smokey would be all right, despite our original fears.

When my oldest son got married and moved to another state, I decided it was time for me to fill my emptying nest with another cat. As many cat owners do, we went to a shelter to adopt a cat who needed a home, and seeing two tiny kittens, each alone in a cage, we decided to adopt both of them. We needed them, they needed us, and they needed each other.

It turned out Cleopatra had needed them, too.

We had originally adopted Cleopatra to be a playmate for Smokey and Bumper, but neither of them ever really played with her or paid much attention to her. With these new kittens, Cleo's life suddenly became active and entertaining. It was as if she thought we had brought them home especially for her. We observed Cleo's maternal instincts kick in as she cleaned them and watched over them. When the kittens were playing with each other, she would often find the highest point in the room, on top of the TV or another piece of furniture, and supervise her babies as they wrestled and pounced on invisible prey. Though older and larger than the new kittens, she was still a kitten herself, and sometimes she joined in the swatting and chasing.

However, when playtime was over, Cleo and the two kittens were drawn to Smokey, our old man. It wasn't unusual to see all four cats cuddled up in a large pile on a small piece of furniture, with legs, bodies, and heads twisted and overlapping. It was hard to tell where one cat stopped and another began or whose tail was whose.

What we had not realized or anticipated was what the two new kittens would do for Smokey. Once shy, Smokey became the patriarch of the pack. If Smokey got up to eat, the kittens would follow him. We even had to get a larger bowl because all four cats insisted on eating at the same time. If Smokey got up to look out the window—a new discovery for our old man who had spent the first ten years of his life under a bed—the others would be by his side learning from him. Once Smokey decided to take on this new role, it was as if he'd always known how to do it. We were amazed at how quickly and easily he adopted the personality of the wise, elder brother who was there to educate his younger siblings, to teach them how to really be cats and make sure no one broke the rules.

Today, Smokey no longer hides. He seems to understand how important he really is. He has even taken to regularly stretching out across my legs or sitting in my lap at night while I watch TV. Unfortunately, when he crawls into my lap, the other three kitties try to do the same thing at the same time. I suppose I could get up and let them have the chair to themselves, but having Smokey cuddled on my lap is a wonderful new part of my life—even if he does come with his purring entourage!

Itty-Bitty Kitty

By Nancy Edwards Johnson

A few weeks ago, my husband called home from work. My daughter, Jennifer, answered the phone. "Mama, Daddy says that for three days now the men have been hearing a kitten cry somewhere in the garage. This morning they found an orange tabby hiding in a box. Now it's trying to follow them around. It's too tiny to eat on its own. They want to know if we'll come get it before it starves."

With three cats in the house, we didn't need another one. We'd found our oldest, Miss Kitty, in a parking lot when she was a few days old. Her tiny eyes were still closed. We nursed her with a syringe every two to three hours around the clock. When she felt its hard surface touch her mouth, she grabbed it with both paws, nursing noisily until the milk was gone. We knew the troubles of playing mama cat. That didn't stop us from going for the kitty.

"Just remember," I warned Jennifer on the drive to the garage. "Your dad said we can't keep this cat, and I agree. We've got too many now. We'll raise it to weaning size and find it a home."

We pulled into the driveway in full agreement. Before my

daughter shut off the motor, we heard the kitten's yells. The men had placed it, along with a saucer of sugar water, in a box just outside the garage door and left. The poor little thing was yowling a loud protest. If the mama cat had been anywhere around, she'd have heard and come running. Something must have happened to her to abandon a kitten so young.

Jennifer reached for the palm-sized kitten and lifted it out of the box. It curled up in her hand. I just had to hold it. I took it from her, and it snuggled against my fingers and started licking my wrist. Huge blue eyes stared up at me from a tiny bone of a face. Its neck was the same size around as my thumb.

We took turns cuddling the kitten, trying to comfort it, but it kept up its yowling. Jennifer placed it on the ground. Waddling and graceless, it traipsed back and forth between our feet.

"Surely this kitten belongs to someone to be so friendly and unafraid," I commented, walking to the car with the tiny kitten snuggled up against my breast. But I knew that if it was not fed, the little beggar would starve to death.

I cuddled the warm speck of fur as we rode home. The tiny vagrant snuggled under my chin. Then it slipped down my chest and looked up into my eyes, screaming. We headed straight to the vet for kitten supplies.

The vet's assistant checked the little orphan between loud yells. "What an itty-bitty kitty! Seven-tenths of a pound. There's nothing wrong with her lungs. Most cats this dark orangey-red are male, but she looks like a girl. Tiny as she is, it's hard to tell."

We left the vets with syringe, worming medicine, and kitten formula. Itty Bitty had just cost me thirty bucks.

Once home, we walked through the front door with Itty Bitty. Our other three cats gathered, squalling and spitting. I watched them, especially the male, not sure how he'd handle the waif. The tiny orphan faced the full-grown cats, fearlessly continuing to yell.

While I refereed, Jennifer mixed formula and loaded the syringe. I expected the kitten to get a taste of the milk and grab the syringe with both paws as Miss Kitty had. But when Jennifer held it to Itty Bitty's lips, the little ingrate stubbornly locked her jaws. After a five-minute struggle, Jennifer gave up. "Here, you try. She's the most stubborn little thing I've ever seen."

Maybe she hadn't got a good taste. I squirted a dab of the formula on her tiny lips. She glared and clenched her jaws. The only time she relaxed them was to let out a squall. The other cats watched, worrying and not sure if they should slap the kitten or me.

Frantically, I glanced into the cupboard for a bowl. The kitten was too short to reach over the rim. I squirted a few drops of the formula directly onto a floor tile and stuck the kitten's nose in it. She got the idea and started licking the floor, making loud smacking sounds with her tiny mouth. I repeated the process until there was not a drop of milk left.

With her belly as hard and round as a golf ball, Itty Bitty stopped yelping. When I picked her up, she climbed my chest and cuddled under my chin. With a satisfied burp she purred with as much enthusiasm as she had squalled.

By the next day Itty Bitty had diarrhea. The formula did not agree with her, so it was back to the vet for another brand. That made the kitten worse. By Saturday morning she could hardly stand, and the vet was closed. I was sure the tiny mite would expire.

Luckily, a good friend had ties with a vet. She contacted him, and he suggested feeding the kitten ground liver. After a trip to the store and a meal or two, Itty Bitty was back on her feet.

Relieved and happy to see the kitten eat, I fed her every time she yelled. Soon, each time I walked by the refrigerator, she yelled. If I didn't respond as fast as she wanted, the yelling intensified. The other cats stared and growled, waiting for me to shut her up. Strangely enough, even though they loved liver, they left the kitten's food alone.

The next day, Itty Bitty began to explore the house. When she neared the stairs leading from the living room down to the foyer, our male cat positioned himself between her and the steps and growled. When the kitten protested and tried to go around, the huge tom grabbed her by the nape of the neck and carried her to the safety of the couch where he held her down with his paws and gave her a bath. By the end of the week, all three cats were taking turns bathing Itty Bitty.

Anytime I moved, the little stray followed. If I went outside, she rode on my foot. Getting her tail or paw stepped on did not break her from this habit. She'd look up with huge blue eyes, now changing to gray, and hold up an accusing paw. After a hug, she'd be back riding my foot.

As tame and loving as she was, I became afraid she had belonged to somebody and we'd carried her off. I talked to our friend at the garage and asked him if he was sure the kitten did not come from someone's home. "No," he assured me. "The mama was a stray. I'd seen her roaming behind the house several times, once or twice carrying the kitten. That cat knows you saved her life, and she's paying you back with love."

My friend must have been right because, to this day, the adoration in Itty Bitty's eyes is hard to deny. Most of the time, if she's not sitting on my chest watching me type, she's beside the keyboard, tiny paws pressing keys and little mouth moving with yowls for me.

One by one, that miniscule stray has wormed her way into all of our hearts. My husband was the last holdout. "You're going to have to find that cat a home," he declared, not very enthusiastically, when Itty Bitty came running into the kitchen wailing for food while we were eating.

I just rubbed her head and laughed. "As far as I'm concerned, she has one."

Me? Afraid of a little dog?

Napping can be a full-time job,
if you play it right.

Poised and ready to lasso a mouse.

Hm, I had this strange dream about a rabbit.

A cat's eyes adjust automatically to changing light conditions.

The tipped ear on this gorgeous cat marks him as a neutered feral in managed cat colony.

Even the Spynx cat has a little fur—more like peach fuzz, really.

"Tuxedo cats"—known for their
black-and-white markings—
are perennial favorites.

Homecoming Queen

By Vanni Cappelli

Kabul, Afghanistan, the ruined capital of a tragic, war-shattered land, is a harsh place to live for both human beings and animals. It is no place for a kitten, let alone a motherless and lost one.

As a freelance journalist based in Kabul throughout the summer of 2002, I had just concluded an interview with a member of the Afghani government and was making my way by foot across the city. An American man on these streets drew very little attention. After decades of foreign occupation, first by the Soviets and then by the allied forces led by the United States, the Afghanis had become used to seeing foreigners all over their country.

That day, I was walking up Chicken Street, Kabul's most colorful commercial thoroughfare and a street practically bursting with rugs, gemstones, and ornamental antique weapons, when I heard a faint, plaintive meowing to my left. Following the sound to its source, I was confronted with a heartbreaking sight.

Tangled up inside what looked like a discarded air conditioner was a tiny, pretty tuxedo kitten, wide-eyed, crying out, and pawing the air. I had always loved cats, so without thinking twice, I stooped over and carefully extracted the kitten from the ruined machinery, noticing that it was a girl, as I plopped her into my carry bag. I walked back to the guesthouse where I stayed, the kitten mewing all the way.

I bore her up the stairs and into my room, set her on my bed, and gently stroked her. At first she hissed and struggled, but soon she sat quietly, looking at me with saucer eyes that seemed to express profound terror and intense curiosity at the same time.

I knew from the first that a little girl kitten rescued in Afghanistan should be named Queen Soraya—Afghanistan's first liberated woman. Her appearance in the capitals of Europe dressed in the flapper style of the age enraged the conservative Afghans of her day, and was a contributing factor to a revolution by Muslim fundamentalists in 1929. Yes, this feisty, self-assertive, and very curious girl kitten would be named Queen Soraya.

Over the next few days, little Queen Soraya's fearfulness shifted to "friendly aggression." To put it simply, she acted like a nut; quiet periods of rest were suddenly shattered by manic frenzies during which nothing and no one was safe. Jumping onto my desk, knocking over my books and writing materials, she would then pounce on me and alternately bite the nape of my neck and lick it as I wrote my observations of the reality around us. Queenie, as I began to affectionately call her, seemed determined to prove that she was a true Afghan, wild and spirited as a bucking colt.

Even so, within a few weeks, life with Queenie settled down to a steady, though staccato rhythm. This state of relative calm was disrupted one day when I found myself covering the gruesome aftermath of a car-bomb explosion that occurred the same day as an attempt on the life of the Afghani president. The never-ending violence and human suffering disturbed me deeply. Going home that evening, I entered my well-ordered room. Queen Soraya slept on the bed, soft, dainty, and perfect in her absolutely childlike repose. I have covered wars on three continents and have no problem with exposing myself to danger, but the welfare of those dependent on me is another matter. "I am taking you out of here, Queenie," I said as I stroked her gently purring form. "I am taking you home."

Easier said than done. Anyone attempting to transport a street-found kitten out of a war zone and across half the globe encounters numerous obstacles along the way, any one of which can kill the effort in an instant. Customs rules, policies of individual airlines, and daunting logistics are enough to make one abandon the effort at the outset. But Queenie was family by now, so I devoted myself entirely to the task.

My friends told me that getting her a rabies shot with a certificate of proof was the first necessity; she could pass no international border without it. Also, the fewer airline flights and transfers home the better, since a single, unsympathetic clerk could ruin everything.

I managed to get Queen Soraya her rabies shot, but there are no direct civilian flights from Kabul to the West; most people fly to Islamabad, Pakistan, before going on to their final destinations. I could get a U.N. flight from Kabul to Islamabad but knew it would be difficult to get the required papers from the Ministry of Agriculture, and I was unsure whether the U.N. flights even allowed cats on board.

Then another one of those lucky breaks that marked Queen Soraya's life occurred.

A friend announced over cups of green tea one afternoon that he was driving from Afghanistan to Pakistan. "Why don't you and Queen Soraya come along?" It would be a dangerous, day-long journey, but I was delighted to accept the offer.

The day of our trip dawned cool and clear. My friend and his driver picked me up, and I settled into the backseat with Queen Soraya at my side. We carefully navigated the precipitous heights of the Kabul Gorge east of the city, and in time we came to the Afghanistan-Pakistan border crossing, where our passports were processed as I held Queenie under one arm. "And where is the passport for this little one?" The customs officer smiled, speaking entirely in jest. I fished out her U.N. vaccination book, and he responded with a hearty laugh, waving us on.

No westerner is permitted to cross the Tribal Areas of the Pakistani Northwest Frontier without a Pakistani soldier riding in his car as a guard. And so, a member of the famed Khyber Rifles, the legendary unit that has held the Pass since the time of British rule, was duly assigned to us. Entering our vehicle, the elite rifle-man gave Queenie a surprised look and asked what I was doing with her.

"She is my cat," I replied. "I am taking her to Islamabad, and then on to America."

"To America?" he practically gasped. "You must love her very much."

"Yes, I do," I said with a nod.

Patting her on the head, he asked, "What is her name?"

"Queen Soraya," I said. "The name of a famous queen of Afghanistan."

"Then she shall have an escort fit for a queen," said the Khyber rifleman, shouldering his arms and sitting erect as our "royal" entourage proceeded through the steep and winding countryside. We reached our guesthouse in the Pakistani capital long after nightfall, and Queenie and I both plopped down onto the bed for a much-needed slumber.

The flight to Lahore the next day went smoothly, Queen Soraya in her cage riding in the unoccupied seat next to me. But as we moved to board the final leg of our journey to New York, the trip took a nightmarish turn.

The customs officials demanded to see an exit permit signed by the Ministry of Health. I knew of no such requirement and asked why I hadn't been informed of this in Islamabad. I showed them the vaccination booklet, but it was waved aside. A long argument followed, with various officers consulted and the usual stock bureaucratic responses uttered. Finally they waved us through, and I breathed a sigh of relief.

But it wasn't over yet. Then the clerk at the check-in counter demanded 6,000 rupees (about a hundred dollars) for the special service of accommodating the kitten. By now I was dead broke, with just enough cash for transportation home when I arrived in America. Why hadn't this been mentioned when the ticket had been purchased, and I'd declared that I was bringing a cat? Frustration and fear grew. The obstacles—bureaucratic assertions, bad information, and my lack of funds—began to pile up, increasing the grim possibility that Queen Soraya would not be coming to America.

"All right!" I shouted. "I rescued this kitten from the devastated streets of Kabul, and if I turn her loose here in Lahore she has a much better chance of survival. I will have at least done her that favor. I don't have the money on me, and that's that."

Urgent consultations followed among the Pakistan International Airline officials. By now the departure time was less than twenty minutes away.

Finally, the clerk approached me. "It hurts us very much that we should seem to be denying you this little kitten that you love so much merely on account of money," he said. "Yes, she can go, and you can pay the airline later, after you have returned home to New York."

As we proceeded up the ramp, I reflected that Queenie's stars were indeed lucky ones.

Today, Queen Soraya is a happy, healthy, curious, and still completely nutty cat who has adapted without difficulty to her new home on the banks of the Hudson River in New York. She eats anything, as might be expected of a little one rescued from the streets of Kabul. At Thanksgiving she wolfed down tortellini, turkey, and pumpkin pie; on Christmas Eve she devoured every piece of fish put before her.

Every morning she leaps onto my bed to wake me up, alternately biting the nape of my neck and licking it, telling me that no matter what good or ill may come, nevertheless I must get up and face the day. For although she is an American cat now, she retains the strong spirit of her regal namesake and her Afghani heritage.

Fallen Angels

By Isabel Bearman Bucher

The first time I met my treasured friend Lorraine was in the spring of 1967. Pregnant with my first daughter, I was as big as the house we'd just moved into and was in the act of snitching the huge pink roses that had fallen over the wall between our two yards.

"You can come and take more over here," a voice said out of the blue.

I gasped, unaware that she was even there, and mumbled something about the roses being so beautiful and how I hoped she didn't mind since they'd slipped over the wall and into my hand. I hid the scissors behind my back.

"I'm so glad you rescued my fallen angels," she returned with that quiet chuckle I grew to love so much. It was a term I'd hear again, one she used to describe finding something precious you thought you'd lost.

Lorraine was a struggling, newly divorced mother of four then; I was a young wife and soon-to-be new mother. As the years passed, we grew close; we shared life on a regular basis as the kids grew up and moved out. She saw me through the death of one husband and on to another marriage to a wonderful man.

One day she called me over.

"I went to the Animal Humane Association because I wanted to check out volunteering," she explained, as I gaped at the biggest orange cat I'd ever seen. "I never thought . . . but the minute he put his paw out of the cage . . ."

Like a female Noah, Lorraine had nurtured a boatload of snakes, rats, betta fish, iguanas, and even a ferret, because her brilliant kids had insatiable appetites for knowledge and a taste for unusual pets. But this was her first cat.

From her lap, "Othello" locked onto me with half-closed butterscotch eyes, as he waxed content under her gentle hand. For her birthday a few weeks later, her grown kids gifted her with an addendum: "Ashly." In the space of two weeks, Lorraine went from zip personal proprietorship to being owned by two cats. Quiet and small, named for the color of ashes, this kitty would show me another side to my gentle friend. While Lorraine had always been the kind, loyal pal who never failed to bring sense and reason when I'd lost mine, this kitty brought out her true nature—an almost irrational, never-give-up stance in the face of what other folks would call hopeless odds.

Her test started on a cold, bright Southwestern day around Christmastime, when Ashly got out of the house and took off, as cats sometimes do. Twenty-four hours later, she hadn't come home. Lorraine put an ad in the paper and visited the Humane Association and the animal shelter every day. Sick with worry, she checked the log our city shelter puts out: a list of all the dead animals found and where they were picked up. She also distributed handwritten notes to more than forty houses in the neighborhood, describing her cat and providing her phone number. Kind people called, saying they'd lost a cat, too; they sympathized about how much it hurt and promised to keep a sharp lookout. Eight days and a dozen shelter visits later—plus one more walk to all the houses to make sure people had gotten the note—she was trying to accept that her cat might be gone for good. Without feeling the least bit of Christmas spirit, she went to get her boxes of Christmas decorations out of the crawl space under the house where they were stored. Checking inside the boxes, she realized with a jolt that the bright angel, always the first on the tree, wasn't in its usual place. In the near dark, she made a frantic search for the cherished ornament. Finally, she spied it, almost invisible, lying intact on the ground: another fallen angel.

Turning it in her hand, Lorraine thought back to the cool December day when Ashly went missing. She reasoned that many people were out raking leaves, closing down gardens, and readying their houses for winter that day. A curious cat just might find a cozy crawl space or garden shed irresistible. And so, she revisited all the houses again, or left notes, asking if people would please check their crawl spaces and garden sheds.

Later that afternoon, she received a call from a woman who said she thought she'd heard a cat meow under her house, but added that the neighbors had a very noisy cat and a new baby, and that's probably what she had heard. She went on to explain that her exceedingly heavy crawl space cover had been off for a couple of hours the day Ashly had disappeared because her furnace was being worked on. Lorraine asked permission to come with her son, just to take a look.

The sun had already set by the time they arrived at the house. Literally taking a last shot in the dark, Lorraine's son hauled off the heavy cover and made his way into the crawl space, flashlight in hand.

Lorraine bent down to look in the opening. "Ashly! Ashly!" she called, hoping against hope, while the neighbor looked on, shaking her head. A minute later, Lorraine thought she saw something catapult by her. In the dark, she couldn't be sure. She even thought she might be imagining things, because by now, she'd been hoping for so long.

Emerging empty-handed, Lorraine's son turned to the woman. "Thank you so much," he said softly, knowing his mother was close to tears. "And, by the way, you've got a leaky water pipe under there."

They walked home, still calling and searching. With a sinking heart Lorraine realized that whatever had shot past her—if anything really had—probably wasn't Ashly.

Arriving home sad and disheartened, Lorraine thanked her son, said good night, and headed for the back door. The minute she reached her back porch, *Wham!* Ashly hit her chest like a freight train, alternating yowls and purrs so deafening they made Lorraine's hearing aids buzz. She just held her close, petting and speaking to her softly, until she realized that she'd been standing on her steps for a long time.

The next day, the skeletal cat ate and drank sparingly every half hour. Lorraine knew that under extreme survival situations, animals go into shock and can often enter a kind of hibernation, but that leaky water pipe probably saved Ashly's life.

"You never gave up," I told my friend one afternoon just before Christmas, as two contented cats curled up, warm and purring, in our two laps.

"Well, I just had to try everything," she said, with a smile. "Fortunately, I had a reminder from a *real* fallen angel." She nodded at the Christmas tree and its uppermost ornament across the room. "But most of all, I had to think like a cat—a curious one, the color of ashes, with eight lives left."

The following spring when Lorraine was having her flat roof replaced with a pitched one, she caught just the barest flick of the color of ashes disappearing into a hole in the ceiling that the roofers were just about to close.

"Oh, no, you don't!" she hooted, drawing the attention of the roofers. Up the ladder she scampered and stuck half her body into the space to pull out that about-to-be fallen angel. "You're forbidden, forever, to subtract any more of your lives! Eight it is, Miss!"

Ten years later, Erica, my now forty-year-old daughter, moved into a lovely new home. One of her three cats, Zanny Z, went missing the first day. Erica knew never to let her cats out of any new digs for at least two weeks, but with all the toting of boxes the cat had escaped unnoticed.

"Remember Lorraine's fallen angels," I said gently when she called, crying. "Don't give up! Make notes; put them on every door. Take out an ad in the paper. Walk the neighborhood. Bang on doors. Do it over and over. Think like a cat."

But no one had seen Zanny Z anywhere.

Twenty days later, Erica received a cell phone call when we

were having a girls' day out shopping. She started hooting, tears filling her eyes.

"Yes! I've got it," she said, frantically rummaging in her purse for paper and pen. "We're on the way!"

Zanny had gotten into a potting shed belonging to people on the route back to her old house.

"I read your notes," the lady said, when we arrived. "I went out and checked my shed, just in case, and didn't find anything. But today I thought I heard faint yowls—and there she was! She must have been living on the cockroaches and mice out there and the water left in the watering cans."

How many fallen angels have been rescued by the never-give-up resolve of loved ones? Bless my friend for her lesson, bless good people for their kindness, and bless curious cats who do what it takes to endure through the worst of times to come home, safe and sound, once again.

celebrating the Bond

You're Invited to a Kitten Shower!

By Roberta Beach Jacobson

Meg and her husband were devastated when the doctor gently informed them they could never have their own children. On the way home from getting the news, they saw a sign at a veterinarian's office, stopped, and adopted a boxful of abandoned kittens in need—four balls of tigery fluff, about three months old.

The kittens lifted their spirits and kept them busy. Meg readily admitted their nine-year-old Siamese, Ming, had been spoiled rotten, and she vowed to do the same with the newest members of their household. None of the kittens had names. Pondering what to call them, Meg had a great idea: she mailed out about a dozen invitations to friends—to a kitten shower! Guests were not to bring presents, but rather ideas for names.

Of course, every one of us arrived at the shower bearing small gifts for the adorable American shorthair kittens; everything from Ping-Pong balls to practical items such as cans of cat food and sacks of kitty litter. None of us had ever been to—or even heard of—a kitten shower. As we munched on healthy snacks, Meg explained how the naming process would go. She passed around sheets of paper, one to each of us. Meg told us there were three male kittens and one female. So everyone was told to suggest four kitty names, only one of which could be gender-specific. We were instructed to tear our papers into quarters and write one name on each piece.

And so we started writing and ripping, as well as whispering and laughing. No cat I ever knew could boast such a flurry of activity over being named. At the time of their naming, all four kittens were sound asleep in their basket in the kitchen, oblivious to the friendly competition taking place in the living room on their behalf.

Finally, all of our suggestions were collected, the papers folded, then put into a plastic container. Meg shook it, and then she shook it some more. Though none of us wanted to admit it, we were all twenty- and thirty-something *kids* eager to win, hoping to have one of our names selected.

She drew the first name. "Let me adjust the microphone," she joked, as she stood up to make the announcement. "Ladies and gentlemen, the first kitten is named . . . Squeaker!" She waved the little slip of paper.

Two women jumped up, both claiming the idea.

Meg was laughing at us so hard she could hardly continue. "Kitten number two is . . . Cashew!"

We clapped as the man who suggested Cashew stood up and took a mock bow.

Meg put her hand into the container again and fished out another slip of paper. "I'm happy to announce kitten number three will now be known as . . . Sam-Sam!"

The woman seated on the couch next to me almost knocked her salad bowl onto the rug as she jumped up in victory. Her cheering alerted Ming, who peeked around the corner to investigate the cause of all the commotion. Apparently the noise was too much for her, as she quickly retreated.

Meg picked out the last name. "Oh, no! It's Rumpel . . . Rumpelstiltskin!"

The man who'd suggested Cashew was able to take a second bow. For him, and for us all, it was an unusual celebration, one to remember for years to come. None of us ever figured out how Meg and her husband decided which kitten got which name, but they managed somehow.

It's now five years down the road, and Squeaker, Cashew, Sam-Sam, and Rumpie are adult cats who love their big sister, Ming. Most of the time they all get along fine, except for the occasional sibling rivalries.

Usually I have a hard time remembering the names of friends' cats. Since the selection of these kitties' names was so personal, they remain clear in my mind. I've never understood how monikers suggested by strangers happened to fit the quartet of cats so perfectly. According to Meg, they took to their names immediately—even faster than they figured out the litter box. Her theory is that they were tiny when named, so they've grown into their names. No matter if due to a little luck, or if something more magical was involved, the names remain a comfortable fit.

Recently the felines got another sister in the house, but this time a human. Yes, Meg and her husband adopted a toddler! This time, however, they opted to come up with a name without the input of well-meaning friends. As Meg told us, "Please! We don't need another Rumpelstiltskin in the family!"

Eight-Pound Privilege

By *Teresa Hoy*

Her eyes were large and round as I lifted her to replace the newspaper and towel she lay on. Such deep blue eyes. I seemed to read numerous emotions in them—the main one, trust. I stroked her head and whispered, "It'll be okay," into her soft fur before setting her back into the cage.

I latched the cage door, wondering what lay ahead for her. She was a five-year-old Himalayan named Sheena, barely a lapful of creamy-colored fur, tipped with tortoiseshell brown. She had been brought to the animal clinic where I worked as a veterinary technician. Though she couldn't talk, her injuries explained the whole tragic event. She was the victim of a gunshot that had left a pellet lodged in her spine, paralyzing her hind legs. The doctors hoped that once the swelling receded around her spinal cord, she might regain the use of her legs.

A couple of weeks passed, but nothing changed. We learned that her family didn't want to care for a disabled cat, but I couldn't stand the thought of her just being discarded. With the family's permission, I took her home with me to give her spinal cord more time to heal. It never did, and the paralysis remained.

Her front feet had been declawed long before I came to care for her. Defenseless except for her teeth, she was now completely dependent on me.

At the beginning of our relationship, there were moments when I questioned my decision to let her live an invalid's life. *Was I doing the right thing for her?* I asked myself this question repeatedly while watching her pull her lifeless lower body and legs across the floor, her tail dragging limply behind like a fur boa. I studied her for signs of distress, depression, or pain. I prayed for answers. I sought advice from my veterinarian.

Then one day I began to feel differently about her. The pity I had felt faded away, leaving only love and the belief that she wanted to live. When I held her in my arms, she would gaze up at me with her big eyes. She would wrap her front paws with their long tufts of dark hair firmly around my arm, as if to tell me she didn't want to let me go. Her eyes would close, and her purring would fill the room. I soon quit doubting my decision. She was strong and healthy except for the paralysis, and she seemed to be enjoying her life. I would care for her as long as she needed me.

I learned to manually squeeze her bladder to empty it twice daily because she could no longer urinate on her own. This meant that if I stayed overnight anywhere, I usually took her with me. As a result, Sheena has traveled far in her lifetime. She has wakened to the sound of water slapping the shores of the Great Lakes. She's been to the beaches of Florida, the mountains of Colorado, and most states in between. For these trips, the backseat of the car becomes her own personal traveling quarters, complete with pillows, blankets, food, and water. For the last eight years, she has been constantly by my side and I by hers.

"How do you do it?" a friend asks.

"Commitment," I reply. "I made a commitment, and I'm happy to keep it." I imagine it's how a mother feels about her child. You do what has to be done.

Sheena and I have come to know each other well. When you live with an animal every day, you learn to see beyond the differences in your bodies, your outer shells, and you look instead at the inner spirit. When I look at Sheena, I see her needs are not so very different from my own.

As with any two individuals living closely together, we don't always agree. Sometimes I will want her to sit on the sofa, and she'll want to sit on the floor. I might need a moment to myself right when she needs me to hold her and scratch her ears. There have also been minor medical problems that have tried our patience, but we never give up. We're in this together and will be until the end.

It no longer troubles me when I hear people say, "The poor thing," or "I feel so sorry for her." It's not that I want her to live a paralytic life; I would trade all the years of knowing her if she could walk on four strong legs again. However, Sheena has adapted to her physical restrictions and has learned to live a good life in spite of them.

Now in her fourteenth year, Sheena needs a little extra care, a little gentler touch, as her lower body loses muscle mass, and her backbone rises up like a small ridge of mountains, becoming more tender. She spends most of her days lounging around on my bed, the sofa, or in front of the woodstove when the weather turns cold. She still has a voracious appetite, and though her dry food is always within reach, it's her breakfast and supper of canned food that bring her into that peculiar sitting-up position where her back legs stick straight out between her front legs.

Her voice is but a whisper, yet I can hear it in the middle of the night if she calls me. When I enter a room where she is sleeping and say, "Sheena?" her head will rise in recognition.

All these years, I thought I was taking care of her, but I've come to realize she has been caring for me as well. Her tranquility soothes me during anxious moments. Just holding her warm, purring body can cause tension to drop away in an instant. Sheena has also been teaching me patience and the value of putting others' needs first—lessons I needed to learn most.

She may be small, just eight pounds, and pitiful in the eyes of some, an encumbrance to others, but to me she is a rare, unexpected blessing. It's been my privilege to care for her and love her.

Our coming together was by tragedy, and our separation will be painful, but our journey together has been extraordinary.

The Not-So-Calico Cat Comes Home

By Gina Spadafori

My dad hated cats, my mom was allergic to them, and my gram, who took care of us kids after school, was afraid of them. If a cat tried to rub against her, she'd shriek.

The odds were definitely not in my favor when I answered everyone who asked me what I wanted for my tenth birthday with a single, consistent answer: "I want a calico cat."

"How about a new softball glove?" said my dad, a strong, graceful, and athletic man, a former professional athlete who held high hopes for all of his klutzy offspring.

"How about a record player?" said my mom, who didn't really like me playing my 45s on their grown-up stereo.

"How about an Easy-Bake Oven?" said my grandmother, who worried that my dad's games of catch with his kids—me and all my brothers—was turning me into what her feminine heart dreaded most, a tomboy.

But I was resolute. "I want a calico cat."

My birthday is just a few days after Christmas—on New Year's Eve, in fact. As is the case for many kids born between Thanksgiving and New Year's, my birthday was usually just wrapped into

the rest of the holiday celebrations. That year, though, I knew
my birthday would be special. A whole decade had passed since
I was born, and my parents had planned a big party to celebrate
it, with all our relatives, friends, and neighbors invited.

Would they give in on the cat under such circumstances? I
wasn't so sure, and so I'd come up with a backup plan: a secret
cat.

It wasn't hard to find a cat in the days when people thought it
normal—even preferable—for pets to roam free. Strays making
their way on their own were common. With the help of leftover
tuna hoarded from dozens of brown-bag lunches, I lured in the
neighborhood contenders and considered my choices.

There was, alas, not a calico among them, and they were a
ragged-looking crew besides. The females couldn't be encouraged
to get close enough to pick up, but a few of the males were more
than bold enough to endure my holding them in exchange for a
bite of my mom's mayo-laced tuna sandwich filler. (My gram's
recipe, with pickle relish, was met with far less enthusiasm.)

Not one of the toms was neutered, and they all walked with
the wide-shouldered roll of cats who'd been around the block a
time or two. Scars and missing patches where fur should have
been were proof of their constant fighting for territory and, perhaps, their scrapping for food as well. I soon had them all running to me at my first call of "kitty-kitty," but none seemed worth
sneaking home.

And then, just around Thanksgiving, a new cat came out when
I called. He was young, too young to have developed the massive
jowls of the older males, and he seemed lonely, confused, and cer-

tainly hungry. Our home was a block from an old cemetery, and looking back, I'm guessing the cat's sudden arrival meant he'd been dumped.

I named him Calico, of course, even though he was just a common gray tabby.

I carried him home and left him behind the shed with the mashed-up remains of my lunch sandwich, plus most of the milk I'd gotten Gram to pour me for an after-school snack. He was still there before school the next morning when I took out the trash and fed him scraps from the bag. (If my mom was surprised that I volunteered for a chore, she gave no sign of it.)

As the rush of the Christmas season enveloped us, no one seemed to notice that I was stealing food. No one seemed to notice, either, that I was spending more time up in my second-floor bedroom, handing that food out the window to a cat who'd quickly learned to come to my call. Cali could kick his way up the magnolia, leap onto the roof, and be at my window in less than a minute.

So sure was I in my deception that a time or two (when the weather was bad), I let Calico sleep on my bed, confident that my parents wouldn't open the door to check on me after they'd gone to bed.

I didn't worry about how to keep Calico hidden—that seemed to be going just fine—but I was dreading the "What do you want for your birthday?" question as Christmas passed and the big party neared. I may have been a sneak, but I wasn't a liar, and I already had my "calico" cat.

But nobody asked.

The morning of my tenth birthday, after my dad made us all his special Mickey Mouse–shaped pancakes, my parents asked me to stay in the little breakfast nook, while my brothers went into the living room to play.

"Your father and I know you want a cat," said my mom.

"A calico cat," I interrupted,

"Yes, well, anyway . . . a cat," said my mom as I waited. "Your father and I talked about this, and . . ."

"You can have a cat," said my dad, "but . . ."

"But . . . ?" I said.

"We need to know where you got that cat," said my mom. "Whose cat are you feeding up there?"

They knew! I quickly considered my options and decided to tell the truth, the story spilling out in a rush.

"You need to put an ad in the paper," said my dad.

"But if we can't find the owner, you can keep him," said my mom.

". . . outside," barked my dad, and then softening, just a little, he said, "What's its name, anyway?"

"Calico," I said.

"But that's not a cali—" Mom started to say.

"Calico," I repeated firmly.

"Calico it is," said my dad. "Happy Birthday, and honey, don't hide things from us again."

"I promise," I said, dying to go get Calico off the roof and already trying to figure out how I could sneak in a dog. And maybe a horse, too.

The classic calico cat is usually—but not always—a female.

You can usually spot a tabby by the "M" pattern on its head.

Snuggling comes naturally to kittens.

A place to perch, perchance
to scratch . . . ideal.

Watching and
waiting are favorite

The influence of a Siamese
is evident in this cat's
lovely markings.

Who needs words? Cats are very capable of making their desires known.

The eyes have it with this cat.

Kitty Bonds

By Samantha Ducloux Waltz

I checked the digital readout on the baby scale I used to weigh Naomi, my beloved cat. Seven pounds, six ounces. "She's lost three more ounces," I wailed. That made a pound and a half in six weeks time.

"Your cat's fine, honey." My husband, Ray, clearly found my daily kitty report less interesting than the biography of Thomas Jefferson he was trying to read.

"She isn't. I know all her blood work was good at her checkup three months ago, but something's changed." I couldn't keep the worry out of my voice.

He set his book down with a sigh. "She's getting older, sweetie."

"Thirteen isn't that old for a cat."

"You don't have anything to worry about. Look at her coat. Look how she acts." He picked up his book again.

Could he be right? Naomi's coat was still a sleek black. She still ran up and down the hall at night, true to our nickname for her, Thunder Paws. She slunk around on the buffet and piano daily, as agile as ever. She was even eating the same amount of food—but there was that weight loss.

I frowned; Ray's absorption in *Thomas Jefferson: A Life* seemed callous to me. On the other hand, I reminded myself, he wouldn't be indifferent to Naomi's health if something turned out to be wrong. He had a kind heart.

If only Naomi would treat him as she did me, I was sure he'd be the first to rush her to a vet. But she treated him like a pariah. She fled every time she saw him. At night, when Ray and I went to bed and turned out the lights, Naomi leapt up beside me and snuggled in. She always slept on the outer edge, never between Ray and me. In the night, when she stirred against me, I unconsciously moved toward Ray to give her room. Again she would stir; again I would move. Ray would awaken, about to fall off the bed, and find me sleeping comfortably on his side of the mattress with Naomi snoring softly beside me. I had it all—Ray's solid bulk on one side of me and Naomi on the other, the softness of her fur against my cheek, a motor that quieted my spirit, and kitty kisses bestowed with her sandpaper tongue. Ray had . . . well, he had a bill for the king-sized bed he bought to keep all three of us comfy.

I often told him it wasn't personal—Naomi treated everyone but me like a pariah. She had humbled every one of our friends and house sitters who claimed they could bond with any cat. Even if they stayed a week, they never saw her, although they did notice food and water disappearing, and her kitty litter box filling. Still, I knew her treatment of Ray must bruise his ego.

"I know you don't like Naomi," I said more gently, "but I need you to help me get her in the carrier, so I can take her back to the vet."

"You're wasting your money on another vet bill. Her only problem is, she's not normal. Normal cats wind themselves around your legs. They sit on your lap. They let you pick them up and pet them. I couldn't touch her to put her in the cat carrier if I tried." He glared over at Naomi peering out from under his chest of drawers—one of her favorite hiding places—and resumed reading.

He was right; Naomi was the original "fraidy-cat." I got the kitty carrier, pried Naomi out from under the chest of drawers with soothing sounds and a firm grip, and took her to the vet by myself.

The next day, after the vet called with results of the blood work they'd done, I found Ray out working in the garden, his favorite activity since his recent retirement. Sadly, he had very few days to putter in the garden or play golf, which he loved. He devoted at least a day a week to visiting his aging mother who had been diagnosed with Alzheimer's and another afternoon with his chronically ill son. Household responsibilities and management of his mother's financial affairs seemed to gobble up the rest of his time.

"Naomi's hyperthyroid," I told him, on the edge of tears.

Ray looked up from pruning a rose bush. "Hyperthyroid? That's not so serious, is it?"

"If we don't give her medication, she'll just keep losing weight and . . ." I left the rest of the sentence to his imagination. I would never be able to give her the medicine by myself. Naomi might snuggle with me in bed at night, but she wasn't about to sit quietly in my lap while I popped little white pills down her throat.

"So something's really wrong," Ray said softly. "Poor Naomi."

I'll do my best to help, but she isn't going to like it."

That night, dressed in a thick fleece shirt to protect himself from her extended claws, Ray cradled Naomi in his arms while I opened her mouth. I barely got the pill in before she arched away from me and somehow scrambled out of Ray's grip.

That night she didn't sleep snuggled against me. The next day she never came out of hiding. In the evening I found her crouched behind the card table in the spare bedroom closet. Again I plopped her in Ray's well-swathed arms and tickled her cheeks and chin till she opened her mouth, then placed the pill well back in her throat.

The third evening I couldn't find her anywhere. This wasn't working!

When I called the vet, he advised that we get the medication in the form of a salve that could be rubbed in her ear. Most cats tolerated that well, and many actually liked it. So I purchased the salve and searched for my cat. I had to remove the towels and tablecloths from the linen closet before I found her hiding in a high back corner.

Ray sat on the bed, his face drawn. It had been one of his days to visit his son. "She isn't going to like this either," he predicted.

"She has to like it," I said and put Naomi in his arms.

Instantly, she leapt away and darted into our closet.

"You have to hold on to her," I said.

"Ya know what? I've had a rough day. I'm just not up to this." Ray took off his shoes, propped some pillows on the bed, picked up his book, and stretched out to read.

I saw the lines of worry etched in his face and the sag of his shoulders, and my heart went out to him. Still, Naomi had to have her medication. "I know you had a hard day, honey, but we have to at least try," I said, giving him a kiss on the forehead and tucking the comforter up around him for protection.

I cornered Naomi in the closet and explained to her in my most comforting voice that we loved her and were trying to help her. She blinked her round yellow eyes at me, her body rigid with tension and fear. "You'll be fine," I reassured her, as I set her on Ray's chest, facing him, and he put his hands on her back to hold her in place.

"You're doing great, both of you," I said as I rubbed the compound into Naomi's left ear.

Ray, for his part, managed to begin tousling her fur with the ends of his fingers as he held her. "See? You're all right," he murmured.

To our surprise, Naomi relaxed, settled on his chest, and turned on her motor.

"She's purring," Ray said, his voice filled with wonder, his frown broadening into a smile. He petted Naomi for perhaps a full minute before she jumped away.

That magic moment became a nighttime ritual. Naomi soon learned that if she jumped on the bed when Ray and I were around, Ray would ruffle the fur at her neck and scratch her cheeks in a way that revved her engine every time. One night I swear I actually heard him say, "I've never been in love with a kitty before. This is my first time."

Their affair blossomed. Naomi began to hang out with us in the mornings. Ray dangled kitty toys for her to swipe at, as I marveled at the change in them both. Their snuggling sessions seemed to relax him. Her coat grew even glossier, and she put on weight, and I don't think it was all due to the medication.

Last night I found Ray in bed with Naomi curled up against him. I could hear her gravelly purr several feet away. It's a good thing we have a king-size bed now, or I might be the one edged out during the night.

Pookie

By Sue Vogan

It was a harsh, cold November. We had lost our beloved Angora cat, Idgy, and my mother had passed away only a couple of weeks earlier. I would have liked nothing more than to have balled myself up and hidden under the covers for a few years, but work was still important if we wanted to have heat and food on the table. Life goes on—or so someone once said.

Our small property management company kept us busy. My husband took care of the maintenance calls; I took care of most everything else.

One sunny but cold morning, a tenant called to inform me that there were two kittens under her home. The weather was supposed to get bad, and she was concerned for their welfare. I told her I would be right there.

With a cat trap (a small cage with a can of food for bait) in the truck, I was off. The drive was short, but still enough time for me to miss my mother again. I was hoping the tears would not sneak up on me before I finished catching the kittens and dropping them off at our local no-kill shelter.

I was in luck. The smell of tuna from the trap lured them out, and both kittens came scampering toward me right away. The white kitten was shy. She stopped short of the cage and watched me closely. The calico kitten made a dash for me. She ran up my leg and snuggled inside my open coat. Her claws dug into my sweatshirt, letting me know she wasn't leaving.

The tenant commented that she had never seen a kitten do that before. She wasn't alone. Having five other cats at my house, I knew this was an unusual situation.

With the white cat caged and the calico still attached, I lifted the cage into the back of the truck. Now, what to do with this little shirt-hugger? I decided to take them both back home and see if my husband could be of some help.

My husband pried the calico from my shirt and slipped her into the cage. I disappeared inside the house to call the shelter's manager and asked him to come and pick up the kittens. I just didn't feel like driving the kittens into town and seeing all those animals without homes. I was depressed enough already.

As I sat at our dining room table, waiting for the shelter manager to arrive, my mind drifted back to my mother, as it did so often lately. Mom would feed the wild birds all winter, cared for strays, and loved her dog, Nikko, with devotion. I missed my mother more than I had ever missed anything in life. My thoughts drifted further back, to my childhood, remembering how my mother brushed my hair each night at her dressing table. Afterward, she heard my bedtime prayers and tucked me into bed. How I longed for those days again.

My husband walked in, ending my reverie, and announced the arrival of the shelter manager. Something inside me suddenly shifted, and I asked him to bring the calico back into the house.

"We already have five cats," he reminded me.

"We have six," I replied firmly.

My husband did not argue. He removed the calico from the cage and brought her inside.

She was not cute. Her hair was long and went every which way, and she looked as if she had been hopscotching on paint cans and had fallen into the brown, orange, white, black, and tan. But the calico didn't seem to feel the least bit insecure or out of place as she jumped down from the sofa and started to investigate her new surroundings. She was being investigated, too. Her new brothers were interested to know if she liked to play. They rolled her around, chased her, and wore themselves out. She passed the test—there was no hissing. We named her Pookie.

Pookie went for shots and spaying; she received her first bath and proceeded to take charge of "the boys." Then, at the end of the first week, something happened that made it clear to me why she had been dropped into my life and why, out of the blue, I had asked my husband to rescue her from the cage.

I'd been feeling low all day and had decided to turn in early for the night. Pookie jumped into our bed just as I was settling in. I laid my head down on my pillow and she curled up next to my ear. She buried her face in my hair and seemed to be brushing it with her front paws. When I began to say my nightly prayers, Pookie stopped brushing—as if she were listening.

That night, I drifted off to sleep, feeling like a contented child again.

Smitten

By Cindy Buck

My husband and I had to travel from two distant planets to meet at the altar and pledge our lives to each other. The attraction was there from the start, yet it was hard for us to make the connection. We were different in so many ways. Despite our wish to come together, our magnetic fields were stuck in repel mode, until a cat bewitched us into love.

Muffin was mine, my first and only cat since childhood. She came to me when I was a single woman in my late thirties. While visiting my friend Meryl in her new home, I learned that the previous homeowners had left their four-year-old cat behind to fend for itself with a large, open bag of cat food in the garage and a cat door to come and go through. Meryl wanted to keep her, but her two kitties had voted no. I was concerned for the cat, but I didn't think much more about it until I was heading out to my car to leave.

There she was on the sidewalk: the most beautiful cat in the world. It was January, the snow was deep, and this kitty had such a thick coat of fur I thought, *Pumpkin. She's as round as a pumpkin.* It turned out that her name was Muffin, and I kept that when, a half hour later, to my astonishment, I found myself taking her home. I didn't know you were only supposed to transport cats in carriers, so there I was, driving down the street with a screaming cat climbing around the car interior, my lap, and even my head. Muffin hated going for rides.

At home, she was a gentle cat, very mature and settled for her four years. She was lovable in all the usual cat ways, but she was spellbinding in her beauty. A short-haired tortoiseshell tabby, she was "just a tabby" the way Cindy Crawford is "just a woman." She had the classic symmetrical markings on her face and flawlessly applied black eyeliner. Her ears were wide-set and tipped with mini-ocelot tufts. Her tail was short and as thick as a bottle brush, though as velvety soft and smooth as the rest of her. Her underside fluffed out in wanton, ruffling waves of white and apricot.

Rob was enchanted by Muffin on his first visit to my apartment. That was a good thing, because we had some trouble finding things to talk about early on. He was an engineer, a pilot, and a logical, well-organized person. I was a writer, an actress, and, let's just say, operating more from the right side of the brain. It took us quite a while to discover our common interests. Muffin was our first. We'd watch a movie on my TV with her between us on the sofa or, later, spread across our two laps, our hands mingled in the dense, lush bounty of her coat.

That coat, that *coat*—it was dreamlike, otherworldly. Multi-hued, multilayered, plusher than the plushest stuffed toy, so thick it practically stood straight out from her body, rich and luxuriant. Its magic lay in what we reverently called "the downy undercoat." The scientist long hidden in me was aroused by this marvel; each individual hair had bands of different colors from base to tip, creating a topcoat of smoky hues too complex to name and a lighter, shimmering undercoat.

Over time, two hearts, both a tad crusty from waiting decades for a beloved, were gradually melted to a fine, sweet goo by the green-eyed gaze, the throaty purr, and the pièce de résistance—the roll-over-and-stretch that revealed the peachy fluff of belly fur, a heavenly pillow on which to lay your cheek, until it wiggled out from under you.

We reveled, we doted, and we fell so far in love that no amount of superficial distance could keep us apart. And so, we got married. It was a challenging transition, but Muffin was there to help us through the rough spots. In the early days of connubial life, she was our refuge, our saving grace. However passionately we might disagree about some things, before long we'd end up snuggling with her on the sofa, maybe watching Seinfeld, perhaps still red-faced from shouting, but nonetheless, now immersed in bliss.

We could be feisty and demanding with each other, but we stood united as her doting parents. *Tuna? Coming, little Muffers. More? Here you go, sweetie. Petting? Come on up here, you good little girl! You want the entire middle of the bed? Let me just skooch over here a little bit.* She took our adoration as her due and rarely asked for attention or affection. She was sufficient unto herself, the sun we happily revolved around.

Rob's work was stressful and highly technical, but every night, another, more playful and creative side emerged, as he and Muffin entertained each other for hours. He invented many games; their favorite was "cat-fishing." Muffin would position herself on the floor on the far side of the queen-sized bed, and Rob would cast a toy mouse tied to the end of a long string in her direction. She'd arc up like a dolphin, snagging it in midair or on the bedspread, then disappear "underwater" again, to prepare for the next cast. Rewind, replay, one thousand times: we never stopped laughing.

One big challenge back then was that I was an inveterate night owl and Rob a cheery morning person. A big motivation for me to meet Rob's strict 10:00 PM bedtime was that it meant sleeping with two toasty critters, as opposed to by myself in the guest bedroom. Sometimes if I missed the curfew, I tried sneaking into bed with them and warming my icy toes against the snoring furnace that was my husband's sleeping body, or under the hot water bottle of Muffin's bulk. After a few of those attempts, Rob took to posting messages on our bedroom door before retiring. One of his favorites read:

Warning!
Fearsome Attack Cat.
Do Not Enter.
Serious bodily injury is likely.

By the time we had to say good-bye to Muffin thirteen years later, we had long since found our footing in married life. I'm sure we would have made it without her, but it wouldn't have been nearly as much fun. She helped us each day with the lessons every kitty gives so sweetly: Don't think so much. Come and play. Feel the warm sunshine. Never forget: you are magnificent.

feline Love

In Their Own Way

By Sabrina Abercromby

Gabriel runs up to me with one of his favorite toys in his mouth and drops it at my feet. With his tail wagging, he looks up at me, his eyes full of excitement and expectation. I pick up the toy and throw it across the room, and he chases after it. Then he comes back and plops it down in front of me again, rolling over for a tummy rub. As I pet him, he begins to drool and purr. Gabriel is my black-and-white tuxedo cat.

My husband, Keith, grew up with dogs, and I grew up with cats. Gabriel is the perfect compromise—a dog in a cat's body! He has eaten several of my shoes and destroyed all of our miniblinds by chewing off the cords. Countless times, I've prepared to wash a load of laundry only to find that he's gnawed holes in my clothes. He's been a very expensive cat, to say the least, but always worth it.

Keith and I adopted Gabriel and his almost-twin brother, Felix, from an animal shelter when they were ten-week-old kittens. They looked alike, but they were completely different. Gabriel was instantly easy to love—full of confidence and personality, always super affectionate. Felix was the opposite—shy and timid. He was only comfortable when he was around his brother and often sat across the room from us. He would squirm if we tried to pick him up, and he'd duck under our hands when we tried to pet him. It took nearly losing one of them to learn that each cat is unique and lovable in his own way.

It happened when Keith and I went on vacation, about a year after we adopted our cats. It was just a short road trip from our home in California to Tucson, Arizona, so we arranged to have our neighbor take care of the cats.

After our first day of driving, we checked into our hotel. The desk clerk said we had a message and handed us a piece of paper.

It said: "Your cat sitter called. No need to worry, but one of your cats is missing."

No need to worry?! I immediately panicked. Which cat was it? I thought of my affectionate, lovable Gabriel, who had been curled up on my lap, purring, just the day before. I couldn't imagine losing him, and although it made me feel guilty, I hoped it was Felix who was missing.

We quickly called our neighbor to find out more details. She told us that when she went over to feed the cats, she had seen Gabriel, but not Felix. She looked around our house to see if he was hiding somewhere, but she couldn't find him. She said she would go back and check for him again.

I was worried about Felix, but hearing that Gabriel was safe, I breathed a sigh of relief. I felt terrible that I could so easily favor one cat. Was it right that I loved one more than the other?

Again and again, Keith and I replayed the details of our departure. While going back and forth from the house to the car, we had left the door open, so there was a chance that he could have gotten out then. We tried to picture the last place we saw Felix, but neither of us remembered seeing him before we left.

I wondered if Felix could survive outside all by himself. He was terrified of everything, so it wasn't likely that a neighbor would see him. I pictured him scared, hiding under a bush, hungry. He still had all of his claws, but he had never had to fend for himself before.

We wondered whether we should turn around and go home. But our trip had already been paid in full and couldn't be canceled. And if our neighbors couldn't find him, would we have any more luck?

The next morning, we called our cat sitter for an update and found Felix was still missing. Then I called my mother, who lives about a half hour away from our house. She drove over and searched for him, but had no luck. Later that evening, my sister, Jennifer, looked around our yard for him, but couldn't find him.

I couldn't get Felix out of my mind. I thought about his gentle nature—how he would wait outside our bedroom door every morning, so he could walk me downstairs for breakfast. He would do figure eights, weaving in and out of my legs, rubbing his head against me while I prepared my cereal. At night, when I brushed my teeth downstairs, he knew I was about to go to bed, so he would linger around the bathroom. Then when I was ready, he would escort me upstairs to bed.

I remembered my many home improvement projects and how Felix was always nearby. He would watch everything I did with such intensity that he looked like he was taking notes in preparation for an important test. While I was tiling our upstairs bathroom, one by one, bolts, caps, and other pieces of the toilet that we removed appeared downstairs. When we caught Felix bringing down a part between his teeth, we joked that he was reassembling the toilet downstairs.

I thought of how inseparable our two cats were—the way they would nap together with their paws and legs intertwined, how they bathed each other and played together. I realized that Felix might not be a lap cat, but he was definitely affectionate in his own way. It was just so subtle that I had never really noticed it before.

The next day, my mother and sister went over to our house together, determined to find him. They searched every inch of the house—in closets, under beds, behind couches, and under tables—but there was no sign of him. Then Jennifer caught a glimpse of something black moving out of the corner of her eye. It streaked up the stairs, and then she heard what sounded like a cabinet door close. She quietly snuck upstairs and peeked inside the cabinet in the hallway. As she opened the door, she saw two wide, glowing eyes staring back at her in the dark. It was Felix! He had been inside the house after all.

Jennifer went back to the kitchen and saw that one of the cabinets above the countertop was slightly ajar. She and my mother put the pieces together and concluded that he had figured out how to get the cabinet doors open and must have been going back and forth between the cabinet in the kitchen and the cabinet upstairs, eluding everyone.

I was so relieved to hear that he was okay. Keith and I could finally relax and enjoy our vacation, and we came home refreshed, realizing how much we loved both of our cats. We also learned to always check on their whereabouts before leaving the house!

Tonight, as I sit with Gabriel purring in my lap, I look over at Felix on the other couch. He's at a distance, but I'm okay with that. I love him now for who he is. He sees me watching him, and then he gazes at his brother with what looks like longing in his eyes. He stands up and comes over, trying to appear very casual. He lies down next to me, leaning gently against my leg. As I pet him, he begins to purr. We're all content, each in our own way.

Cat Envy

By Carol Kline

I have a terrible case of cat envy. It stems from a severe lack of cats in my life. Though I am the author of two books about cats, have spent years working as a rescue volunteer for both cats and dogs, and am a dues-paying, card-carrying member of the Cat Writers' Association (not cats who are writers, but humans who write about cats), I am not now, nor have I ever been, in a close personal relationship with a cat.

Hard to believe, and not something I admit freely, especially in the circles I run in. But a lack of cats does not disqualify me from being a cat lover. I adore cats. I admire their beauty, their intelligence, their grace—their Jackie O–elegance juxtaposed with that madcap, playful charm. Their fur sends me into such ecstasy, I'm convinced it should be a controlled substance. And don't even get me started on their purrs. Did you know that purring has been scientifically shown to promote healing? Those Egyptian cat-worshippers knew what they were doing.

I'd be overjoyed to have a cat in my life, but there are—how should I put it?—issues. It's my husband. The poor man has cat allergies that can land him in the hospital. When we're invited to dinner at someone's house for the first time, before I can accept, I have to find out if there are cats in residence. I feel so rude returning their offer of hospitality with the third degree: Do have you any cats? Have you ever had any cats? Is there a chance there are cats in your house that you don't know about?

The odd thing is that not all cats set him off. Even so, it's not the kind of chance we like to take: severe asthma is not pretty. His allergies have put a bit of a damper on our social life, but more distressing than that, they've consigned me to a catless home. (Hey, it's a happy marriage, so things could be a lot worse.)

As a child, I assumed that we didn't have cats because we were a "dog family." When I was born, we had a beagle named Bagel, who, after a long, happy life, was succeeded by Twiggy, a miniature Manchester terrier, whose proportions were reminiscent of a certain British supermodel. Our family lived in a big Victorian house, watched *The Wonderful World of Disney* and *Bonanza* on Sunday nights, played miniature golf every summer, and didn't have cats. End of story.

Then I discovered the truth.

I was around seven years old, and I remember flipping through a family album and seeing a picture of my older sister, Barbara. Thirteen years my senior, she was out of the house and living her own glamorous life before I really had a chance to get to know her. In the eight-by-ten studio portrait, she appeared to be around eight or nine, fresh-faced, smiling, her hair brushed into a shining, curly bob, and in her arms she held a cat. *A cat?* It was a beautiful silver tabby with inscrutable eyes and a white blaze down his nose.

I asked my mother, "Why is Bobbie holding a cat?"

"That was our cat," my mom informed me. "His name was Whiskey."

She said it as though it was no big deal, "our cat," but I remember feeling as though the earth had somehow shifted beneath my feet. I'd thought I knew my family, but now I wondered, *What else aren't they telling me?* Suddenly finding out that we'd had a cat before I was born was the start of my feeling that I could be clueless—a day late and a dollar short—when it came to the important things in life. But that is a story for a different book. The salient point here is that it was also the moment my cat envy officially began.

I asked my older sister and brothers about the cat. I wanted to know all the juicy details. Our father had brought him home, they told me, from where no one knew. He was a tomcat with a taste for battles and the notched ears to prove it. He was also a friendly cat and trotted over to you if you called his name, just like a dog. He didn't have a litter box and would scratch at the door when he wanted to go out—also like a dog. But he was 100 percent grade-A cat when it came to head-bumping and leg-weaving, and by all accounts he was a champion purrer. I discovered he even slept in my older brother's bed at night, a warm, furry presence guaranteed to ward off night frights and cold feet.

"How come we don't have a cat now?" I asked my parents repeatedly, but could never get a satisfactory answer.

"After Whiskey died, we just never got another," they said. "We got Bagel instead—aren't you glad?" Well, yes, I was glad, but did it have to be one or the other?

For whatever reason, we never did get another cat. And then

I was in college and then a twenty-something with no permanent place to bring a cat home to. And then I fell in love with a man who didn't do cats. So there I was, a cat-person-wannabe without a cat—my nose pressed against the glass, looking in.

Now I do what I can to feed my cat cravings. I visit www. cuteoverload.com at least a dozen times a day and check out the many photos of cats being, as advertised, so cute your head could explode. I watch YouTube videos of felines playing the piano, skidding off the end of counters, strutting around in knitted headgear, and riding dogs bareback. I visit my friends with cats and sit spellbound as the gorgeous creatures simply saunter across the room like models on a runway. On my strolls around the neighborhood, I smile at the cats I see lounging like sultans in people's windows, letting the sun warm their fur. And when a cat locks eyes with mine and gives one of those silent meows, I melt. Sayonara, heart.

Keats may not have been describing a cat when he wrote his famous line, "A thing of beauty is a joy forever," but he could have been. I'm drawn to cats, captivated by their slinky allure. I respect them and will do everything in my power to protect them from harm. But mostly I just love cats—even if only from a distance.

Named for the pattern of an ancient cloth, the tabby pattern is the most common of cat markings.

Cats spend most of their lives asleep—or looking for places to fall asleep.

White cats are no less
affectionate than others, but
are more likely to be deaf.

Cats love to play, but yarn isn't the best toy around—it can be dangerous if swallowed.

Even shelter cats who look a little ragged will bloom with adoption into a loving home.

Things are certainly
looking up for this cat.

Even cats have "blah" days.

Note to self: Next time I climb
a tree, have an exit strategy.

Heaven-Sent

By Dolores Kozielski

ather Joe was late. A monk of the Franciscan order, the father was my good friend—and our visiting priest. During the summer months he came often to help say some of the masses. I was waiting anxiously for him to arrive at the parish rectory when suddenly the phone rang. It was Father Joe.

"Where are you?" I asked.

"In the church parking lot," he answered. "I need your help."

Rushing outside, I waved to Father Joe, who was opening his car trunk. By the time I reached him, he had his suitcase unzipped. Packed neatly inside were his brown monk's robes. He reached for them.

"What are you doing with those?" I asked.

"I need my cincture," he said. "That's the braided white cord that gets tied around the waist of my robe."

Hearing a rustling noise, I looked up into a nearby tree. There I noticed a frightened half-grown kitten clinging tightly to a drooping branch. Skittish about coming back down to earth, the kitten, whom I immediately pegged as a stray, meowed relentlessly.

"What are you going to do?" I asked.

"I'm going to rescue this tabby—and you're going to help me,"
he said. "I have an inspiration and know just how we can do it."

Father Joe called up to the kitten, "You'll be down soon, little
kitty." Then handing me the cord, he commanded, "Hurry,
Dolores, tie this end of the cincture to my car bumper."

I did as I was told, wondering what in heaven's name my friend
was up to.

Next, Father Joe hopped up onto the trunk of his car. Reach-
ing his arm up as far as he could, he managed to grab the tip of the
tree limb. Pulling it down, he tethered the other end of the cincture tightly to the branch.

"I'm going to move the car forward very slowly. When the
branch gets lower, grab the kitten," he said.

"Aha!" I said, "Now I get it!"

Father Joe gently pressed down on the gas pedal. The car
inched forward ever so slightly. With clinging claws, the kitten
gripped tightly to the cinctured branch. As the branch got lower
and lower, the scared tabby meowed and meowed. Finally, the
little cat was almost in my grasp.

"Just a wee bit more and you'll be able to reach him," said
Father Joe.

The car had only moved forward a smidge when suddenly, the
taut, braided cord snapped. The tabby was catapulted from the
branch, whizzing up and out into the distant sky. Father Joe shot
from his car. Together we watched the poor kitten sailing off
toward the edge of the church grounds and the neighboring
homes beyond.

"Oh, no!" we cried in unison.

Without hesitating, we darted in the direction of the spot where we thought the kitten might have landed. For what seemed an eternity, we searched the bushes, calling for the missing cat. "Here, kitty-kitty. Here, kitty."

Father Joe kept stopping to listen. "Shhh," he'd say. "Do you hear anything?"

But we didn't hear one blessed meow. Eventually we surrendered our search. We both felt bad, but there was nothing we could do except say a prayer for the fallen feline. Father Joe and I had tried our best to save the kitten; now the matter was in God's hands. Brooding, we walked back to the car in silence.

"What a homecoming," I said, as I helped Father bring his belongings into the rectory. "But I bet the kitten will be okay. They have a knack for landing on their feet."

The next day, I went to the supermarket to purchase my weekly groceries. As I passed from the meat section to the frozen foods, I heard my name being called. "Dolores!"

It was Mrs. Kenney, one of the parishioners. As she approached, I noticed a huge bag of cat food and litter stacked in her shopping cart. This surprised me as I knew from past conversations that she had a disdain for cats. I remembered her story of the stray calico who had ruined her beautiful flower garden.

"Dolores, you'll never guess what happened." Mrs. Kenney could hardly contain herself. "Emily, my six-year-old, has been begging me to get a cat for months, so I finally told her, 'If God wants you to have a cat, you'll have one.' Since then, she's been praying every night, asking God to send her a kitten. Yesterday, we both stepped outside to pick up the toys that were strewn all over the backyard. Suddenly, out of nowhere, a tiny tabby flew out of the sky, landing squarely into Emily's arms. Emily shouted, 'Mommy, look! God's answered my prayers!' It was a miracle. I've never witnessed anything like it in my entire life."

My eyes opened wide. "That's amazing," I said, feeling my cheeks flush a little as I recalled the real story of the cat's origins. At the same time I was relieved, knowing that the kitten was safe and in good hands—Emily's and the reformed Mrs. Kenney's.

When I got home, I called Father Joe immediately and told him about Emily's prayers for a kitten and the tabby plummeting out of the blue into her arms.

We both laughed.

"God works in mysterious ways," said Father Joe.

"This time you're absolutely right," I said. "There's no doubt this kitten was heaven-sent!"

Home Is Where the Kitties Are

By Beth Cato

M y entire world changed when, at the age of twenty, I married my husband, Jason. My introduction to life as a Navy wife was swift and ruthless. The day after the wedding, we packed up all my worldly possessions and began the long trek from California to South Carolina. But not everything can be packed in a cardboard box and brought along.

My beloved family cat, Adventure, remained with my parents and brother. There was never any question of that; Adventure was part of the family. He had been born in that house and had lived his thirteen years exploring and defending those grounds. He was also dying of cancer. Moving away, I had to face the fact that I would probably never see Adventure again.

As Jason and I settled into our sparsely furnished new home, there were more challenges. I loved being his wife, but the days were long and lonely. I had no friends and no one to talk to when Jason was at work. I was in a house of echoes, trying to clean and bake and occupy my time. There was something important missing.

I needed a cat.

I knew I could never replace Adventure. The noble tabby,

dubbed the "Emperor of All Cats" by my brother and me, was without parallel. No, I just needed companions, heirs to Adventure's royal throne. There was a significant problem, though—money, and the lack thereof. We were living on ramen and cake mix.

Our windfall came when Jason's grandparents sent us a check for a microwave as a wedding gift. We chose the cheapest one that would suit our needs, so there was money left over. Money for a cat!

We drove to the SPCA in a nearby strip mall. The room resounded with barks and meows, but I was immediately drawn to a cage that held four kittens: two little white fuzz balls and two black tabbies. One of the tabbies pressed against the front of the cage, desperate and mewing. I scratched the kitten's head through the bars, already falling in love.

Jason nudged me. "It doesn't cost much more to get two kittens," he said, nodding toward the two matching tabbies.

"Are you sure we can afford it?" I asked. We had already figured out the expenses—there would be food, litter, shots, and spaying or neutering—and had just enough money to cover them.

Jason smiled at me. He knew how lonely I was and how much I needed a friend in my new life. "Yes," he said firmly. "Get two."

The employee unlocked the cage and grabbed the kitten that had been begging for adoption. "It's a girl," the woman announced, handing me the little one.

"Hi there," I murmured, cuddling my new baby.

"You want the other one?"

"Yes, let me hold the other tabby," I told her, and placed the little girl kitten in a cardboard caddy.

The other one, a little boy, was not so friendly. He had been perfectly comfortable at the back of the cage, and he bristled at the invading hand. Yowling mightily, he was placed on my shoulder. His claws retracted, but he still stared at me, clearly annoyed. It worried me. Would he mellow? I had encountered vicious cats before, untamed ferals who couldn't be cuddled. But these two were a matched set! I couldn't take one without the other.

"You have a fine pair here," the woman said. "About six weeks old, I'd guess." As Jason paid the cashier, I knelt beside the box, thrilled at our new bounty. The kittens were protesting together now, unaware of their good fortune.

I named them on our drive home. Recalling one of our favorite video games, I dubbed them Palom and Porom, after young twins who assist in saving their planet from destructive forces.

I soon learned that these rambunctious kittens were a destructive force unto themselves. The house was systematically explored and destroyed. Nothing was safe. Receipts were shredded, wedding gift glassware broken, lamps introduced to gravity. We discovered Palom and Porom had fleas; after the flea bath, Jason's arms bore long, jagged wounds for weeks, leading his coworkers to tease him about his wife assaulting him.

But the little pair also brought sweetness and affection. They followed me around during the day, mewing and demanding attention. Porom, the female, was small enough to curl up in Jason's "Dixie Cup" sailor hat to nap. Palom, the male, had a fondness for hair and loved to sit on top of the couch and try to groom my long locks.

As time passed, each cat chose his or her favorite human. Porom chose Jason. She adored him. She cuddled his dirty, smelly socks as though they were soaked in catnip. If Jason sat down, Porom was there, ready to claim his lap.

When Palom chose me, I learned that my initial impression of him had been all wrong. Yes, he could be sullen at times, and he was as loud as a Siamese, but that wasn't the sum of his personality. He loved being near me, not in my lap, but right beside me, within petting and stroking range. I dubbed him my buddy cat.

I found a job working nights and on my days off kept to my routine of sleeping during the day. I would eat lunch at three o'clock in the morning and then play with Palom, rolling balls across the floor or dangling string for his entertainment. On those bleak nights, with my husband sleeping or away on shift, both the kittens helped me get by.

Still, there were more bleak times to come. That November, after battling his illness for years, Adventure was finally laid to rest. It hurt me terribly. More than my marriage, more than my move, the loss of Adventure symbolized the end of my childhood and my old life. But when I was disconsolate, there were Palom and Porom, eager to play, wanting my attention. In my sorrow, I didn't feel like facing them. But it didn't matter how many times I tried to push them away. They wanted in my lap, and they wanted to be loved—and they won.

Military families have to deal with unique hardships, as do their pets. We knew we would eventually have to move, and it would be a stressful endeavor, especially with two cats. Many of my coworkers were military spouses, so I turned to them for advice. They all tried to persuade me to place the cats in new homes and not try to have pets while we were in the military.

They said that, between the frequent moves and the extra expense, it just didn't work.

But I knew I couldn't leave my babies behind. Jason agreed. When it came time to buy a new car, we chose a station wagon that had room for a kennel.

When our orders arrived and another cross-country move was required, I got anxious. How would the cats cope with the chaos of a move? As it turned out, Palom and Porom handled things better than I did. Throughout the long drive to Washington State, the cats were secure in their kennel and mostly quiet, reserving their energy for tearing around our hotel rooms at night. They adjusted to our new home without any quibbles; they had their humans, and all was well.

Through each transition over the next few years, the cats were there. When my husband was deployed—and that deployment extended—I had Palom and Porom to keep me company. When we had a baby, Palom was the one who taught our infant son how to crawl. When Jason decided to leave the Navy, we managed yet another cross-country move, this time with a toddler and two middle-aged cats in tow. Our family was still intact.

The years have passed and Palom is still as loud as a car horn, eats hair like a fine dessert, and likes banging open the kitchen cabinets at five o'clock in the morning. Porom is as fat as a canned ham and the laziest cat I've ever seen, but still as sweet as the first time I saw her in that cage at the SPCA. They are still my babies and as much a part of this family as my husband, my son, or me.

No matter where life might send us, if our two tabbies are there, it's home.

The Cat from Hell's Kitchen

By Gregg Mayer

Polly was an urban cat, found hanging out in Hell's Kitchen eleven years ago when she was under a year old. Hell's Kitchen, just around the corner from my home in Times Square, is an area of midtown Manhattan where for decades Irish, Greek, and Italian immigrants dwelled in the tenement buildings that lined the streets. It was a rough section of town, known for its mix of mobs, gangs, unemployment, and sheer poverty, before it started to come up in the world.

Polly, a pretty little calico, had the temperament to match. But when she didn't like something or had a strong opinion, she sounded like a scolding fishwife, or like Eliza Doolittle in My *Fair Lady*—before her transformation! My neighbor liked to call her "a Hell's Kitchen broad."

At first she was fearful of other cats, probably due to her past encounters in the city streets. But once she felt confident enough to merge with my clan, she got along in a detached way while still preferring the laps of all the resident and visiting humans.

For eleven years, she did her Polly thing, putting up—or not— with the many stray, rescued, or abandoned cats that came in and out of our home. But her special joy was to sit in on the twice-weekly yoga classes I held in my home, a second-floor loft apartment. With its wooden floors, high ceilings, and large windows overlooking the garden in the inner courtyard, the apartment was an oasis of peace surrounded by theaters, shops, and restaurants. Life in New York, as in all big cities, is crowded, busy, and anonymous. The yoga class provided a sense of community for my students and a refuge from the urban experience. It was a place to connect with like-minded souls and with nature—in the form of the courtyard full of trees and my many houseplants and felines.

Polly had a special friend in the class who sat in the same place each time. Twice a week for years, Polly perched on this woman's yoga mat, waiting anxiously for her to appear. She didn't relax till her special friend was seated in meditation. Then Polly would begin to knead on the student's crossed legs and settle into meditation herself. Woe unto us when this student had to miss a session. Polly would wait, craning her neck toward the door, not believing it possible that her beloved person wasn't coming. On those occasions, we all tried to console her, and she had to settle for second best, eventually climbing into some other lap, albeit reluctantly.

Not long ago, I brought Polly to the vet because she seemed not quite herself: her symptoms were varied, but when she didn't come into the room for yoga one day, we knew that something was very, very wrong. She had only been to the vet twice in the eleven years she'd lived with me: to be spayed at six months and to have her teeth cleaned only a month earlier. So I was unprepared when the vet told me how ill she was. Cancer had spread to her lungs, and she had to be put on oxygen. It became clear that Polly—never-sick, never-a-problem, always-there Pollyanna-Polyester—was dying.

I stayed with her for a long time that day. I recited some of the highlights of our life together, starting with my spotting her orange and white calico markings in the bushes on West 39th Street. She seemed grateful that I'd finally recognized her need to be let out of her pain and went to sleep very peacefully. She died as sweetly as she had lived.

A week after her passing, I dreamed I was in a building very different from my own: it had more floors and wasn't at all familiar to me. Polly was in the doorway at my side when suddenly the elevator door opened. A woman I didn't know was standing inside. She said something nice to Polly, who proceeded to walk happily in the direction of the elevator. (She would never have done this in real life, always showing great caution and trepidation whenever the elevator door opened and she happened to be nearby.) The woman encouraged her to enter, and as the elevator door closed behind them, I remember saying something to the effect of "Don't forget to bring her back." The woman laughed pleasantly and responded that she was only going to the ninth floor.

In the dream, I returned to the elevator a few minutes later and noticed that the arrow on the UP button was still lit, but when I checked, there was *no* ninth floor!

Polly, the urban cat, had taken the elevator to Kitty Heaven.

A Penny for Buttons

By Susan Boskat Murray

"**B**ut I have to pay you *something*," I appealed. "I don't feel right *just taking* her."

My veterinarian considered the determination in my expression and grinned. He knew me well, and although others had expressed an interest in the little runt of a kitten that had been abandoned at his clinic, Dr. Jay, as we called him, was just as determined that she would go home only with *me*.

"Okay then," he conceded. "One cent."

And so it was that I paid one penny for a little cat that would change my life—a short-haired meowing machine who made her way into the heart and home of this goal-oriented, workaholic who had no time for "frivolities." Stop and smell the roses? Don't they make an air freshener in that scent?

Around the time she turned four, Buttons became quite ill. The spry in her step grew deliberate and weary, and she often turned away from her food bowl without a nibble. Her favorite perch on the windowsill was abandoned for a plastic stool in the dank and dismal basement. When Dr. Jay detected swollen lymph nodes, he suspected feline leukemia. However, those tests, as well as a slew of others, came back negative. My husband, Tom, and I hopelessly watched our faithful little companion wither away. All we knew was that, with each new blood test, her "packed cell volume" was diminishing, and her bone marrow refused to produce its life-sustaining red blood cells.

Buttons's condition presented me with a major conflict. As the coordinator of a small office, I had always taken my responsibilities very seriously. I made a habit of arriving early and staying late, sure that things would fall apart without me. I enjoyed the intense concentration required to keep my little world spinning, and the satisfaction that resulted from doing so. Now, leaving for work every day was agonizing—how would she fare alone all day?

For a month we took turns driving home at lunchtime and often rearranged our evening plans to make time for the uncomfortable tasks of administering subcutaneous fluids and frequent force feedings. At least twice a week, when Buttons spiked a dangerously high fever, we crashed Dr. Jay's appointment schedule. Buttons was running out of time, and no matter how hard we worked at it, we couldn't seem to give her more. We began seriously considering the unthinkable: euthanasia.

Heading to my car after work one evening, a sparkle on the pavement caught my eye. For some reason, I paused momentarily to pick up what was a shiny new penny. Feeling a spark of hope, I made a wish that my one-cent kitty might survive and emerge as good as new. I tucked that penny into the breast pocket of my jacket, close to my heart, and transferred it to a velvet pouch in my jewelry box as soon as I got home.

Tom and I determined to give Buttons all we were able to give.

We set up a little wooden table near her window so she could lie in the sunshine and breathe in the fresh air while she listened to the twittering birds and watched them flit between the evergreen bushes outside. The shorter, top shelf of the table served as her perch, while her kitty bed, tucked into the cubby beneath, provided a warm cozy den where she could retreat at will.

Over the next few weeks, as I immersed myself in my duties as Buttons's hospice nurse, my dedication to being at the office through "wind and rain and sleet and hail" gave way to a higher calling. Buttons's comfort became my top priority. Though I did what was necessary for the office to keep functioning, I discovered that most of those "urgent" phone calls could wait until the following day, and the reports that had once taken up so much of my attention each evening now sat idle in my briefcase. I routinely spent time each day gently grooming Buttons's dark gray fur and marveling over the wonder of her stark white undercoat. I tenderly scratched her chin and felt her melt under my loving caress as I gave her healing massages. This connection with Buttons, the result of spending my time on what was important rather than what was urgent, filled me with awe.

Time is the one thing no one can buy more of. Buttons helped me see that tomorrow truly is a gift. I'd like to think that our loving care helped to give her almost seventeen more years of tomorrows—happy healthy tomorrows. Yes, she made a complete recovery; and so did I. I not only learned to stop and smell the roses, I planted a *garden*! And at every opportunity, Buttons and I would spend time out in the wafting fragrance of flowers—and catnip. She'd crouch down, close her eyes, and curl up her front paws underneath her chest. In this sphinxlike position, she'd spend time dreaming, meditating, and communing with nature—clearly enjoying every minute. Life is too precious to live any other way.

Buttons would have turned twenty-one on the day I collected her ashes. I've never had, nor believe I ever will have, a cat quite as special. I gave her a part of my life and she gave it back to me, richer and sweeter. Later that day, I gathered her kitty bed from its cubby, and tearfully clutched it to my chest. As I reached inside the cubby to clean, I felt something and picked it up. When I saw what it was, a smile spread across my face despite my tears. You may not believe it, but it's true—there in my palm lay a well-worn, patinaed penny.

Loving Leslie

By Sandra L. Toney

Leslie first came to the local animal shelter as an "unwanted" cat, most likely for one of the usual reasons that cats are given up to shelters: because the cat won't use the litter box or the family is moving to a no-pet apartment. But the ugly truth was that Leslie was now just another homeless face at one of the thousands of animal shelters across this country.

There was nothing special about the three-year-old torbie and white female—except for the fact that she was the sweetest and most loving of cats. Unfortunately, Leslie's chances at adoption were even less than those of other cats because she had an "unsightly" eye, probably due to a serious eye infection as a kitten. The eye itself was very cloudy—it looked almost as if she had a cataract—and the pupil wasn't set in the center of the eye. All of us at the shelter referred to her as "that cat with the odd-looking eye."

Certainly, a very special person would have to come along to recognize her beautiful soul and loving heart. Was that person out there, and, if so, would Leslie ever find them? I knew the odds were stacked against her.

Since I ran the website at the shelter, I also took the photos and wrote the descriptions for all the cats. Trying to help Leslie, I decided to make her the "Cat of the Week" and put her photo in a prominent spot on our website. I was hoping beyond hope that someone out there in cyberspace would see her, read about how affectionate and sweet she was, and be able to overlook her damaged eye.

What happened was something even more wonderful than that.

Ten-year-old Hannah was still grieving for her cat who had passed away last year. Since the cat's death, Hannah's mom, Julie, had felt the family was too heartbroken to adopt another feline. But now Julie was concerned because Hannah was facing another loss: her big sister, Amber, was going away to college in a few weeks. It was the first time that the two would be separated for any length of time. The sisters were very close, more like best friends.

Knowing that it would be hard for Hannah to lose Amber, Julie had been searching for something—anything—to make her daughter happy. When Hannah had made it a point to show both Amber and Julie the "Cat of the Week" photo, Julie knew what that thing would be—a precious kitty named Leslie. Julie came up with a plan to give Amber and Hannah an incredible "bonding" experience. She was going to create a moment so special, neither sister would ever forget it.

The next afternoon Julie stopped by the adoption center I was manning at PetSmart, the national pet store chain. One week a month, the shelter sent cats there, which usually resulted in many adoptions because of the high volume of foot traffic at the store.

Julie told me that her daughter, Hannah, had visited our website and fallen in love with the shelter's "Cat of the Week."

So Julie had come to the store to meet Leslie. When she discovered what a sweet and special kitty soul she was, she knew she was the perfect candidate to be Hannah's new best friend. Julie filled out all the paperwork needed to adopt Leslie, explained the part I would play, and then set the next part of her plan in motion.

She arranged to have Amber and Hannah visit PetSmart later that evening. They were supposed to be just "looking around." When I spotted them, based on Julie's description, I called them over to the adoption area to ask for assistance while I was cleaning the cages. I asked Hannah if she would help me and handed her Leslie to hold while I changed the food and water in her cage.

Hannah immediately recognized Leslie as the "Cat of the Week," and in a few minutes was "telling" Leslie that she would do *anything* to have a cat like her. But, she explained, her mom was too sad to get another one after their other cat had died. Amber was in on the plan, and she and I looked at each other, both touched by the sight of Hannah hugging and cuddling Leslie closely. And "the cat with the odd-looking eye" loved the attention from the little girl—it was so perfect!

At that point, Hannah saw I was finished with the cage and, with a sad expression, turned to give Leslie back to me. It was then that Amber said, "Hannah, you'll break Leslie's heart if you leave her here. I think she wants to go home with you."

Hannah sighed, "Mom said I can't have a cat, so Leslie can't come with us."

Again, Amber suggested that they should take Leslie home and, as before, Hannah replied that she couldn't because Mom would be upset. At that point, Amber pulled out a check written to the shelter and announced, "Surprise! Mom already knows, and here's the check to adopt Leslie."

Then I handed Hannah the application to show her that her mom had already come to the store, met Leslie, and signed all the paperwork. Suddenly, shy, quiet Hannah burst into tears of pure, unadulterated joy. Still holding Leslie, she buried her face in the cat's fur and just sobbed. Then Amber began crying, and even I was so touched, I couldn't keep from crying along with them. It was one of those picture-perfect moments in life—and I was proud to have been a part of it.

As they left, Hannah promised me that Leslie would have a wonderful life with her, and I had no doubt whatsoever that that would be true. The cat with the odd-looking eye was really going to her forever home.

If you're ever about to give up on the demanding job of animal rescue, telling yourself, "I can't do this anymore—it's just too heartbreaking and overwhelming," I hope that you can experience something like this. Something that gives you a small—but oh-so-genuine—glimmer of hope and inspires you to keep finding the Hannahs and Leslies of the world and introducing them to a lifetime of love and happiness with each other.

Cat Rustlers

By Lucyann Murray

"**P**aaaleeeeezzz, Mom, can we keep him?" my nine-year-old daughter, Teri, and six-year-old son, Michael, implored as they stroked the thick fur of a beguiling tuxedo cat. Playful and wide-eyed, the creature already had begun to chip away at the common sense that told me this well-fed feline surely had a home already.

We had recently lost our eleven-year-old dog, Fella, and everyone in the family was experiencing a great sense of loss.

"We can't just adopt a cat that belongs to someone else," I responded to the begging chorus.

"No, Mom," Teri said. "We've never seen him before. He doesn't belong to anyone. I know it! Somebody didn't want him."

". . . or maybe he ran away from mean people, and he needs us," Michael added.

"We don't know that. You wouldn't like it if someone took your pet, would you? And you both have to promise me you won't feed him. If you don't start feeding him, he'll go back to his owner." The children accepted my parental decree but not without loud groans of protest.

Weeks drifted by, and every day the cat showed up on our front lawn, sitting under the mulberry tree with an open invitation to the kids to come out and play. With noses and hands pressed up against the window, they'd shout, "Here he is! Here he is!" At first I told them not to pet or even acknowledge him in any way, but gradually he wore us all down. I checked with all the neighbors on my block, but nobody knew anything about this enchanting little cat.

Soon the kids were calling him Pancake. When I asked why, they admitted they had been feeding him flapjacks squirreled away from the breakfast table while Mom wasn't looking. Neighborhood children also joined in the conspiracy to adopt "Pancake," adding other inappropriate cat chow to his diet, along with an abundance of youthful delight. Pancake sat in their midst, reveling in the attention bestowed upon him like royalty interacting with his subjects.

Finally, I yielded. I convinced myself Pancake had been abandoned and was in need of a good home. "Okay, you win. We can keep him!" Shouts of joy rang out about him while King Pancake sat confidently on Teri's lap. He accepted hugs and kisses between the ears with the patience and dignity expected of a newly crowned monarch. He now ruled our hearts, and he knew it. But trouble lurked just around the corner, literally.

One day, a few months later, as I jogged the neighborhood a few blocks over from my home, an elderly woman came out on her driveway and, throwing up her hands, shouted, "Wait!"

I stopped and smiled. "Hi!" I replied.

The woman just stared at me and then announced, "You stole my cat! I drove by your house the other day and saw you and your kids out playing with him."

The smile froze on my face like sudden winter. I was speechless as my mind raced. Horse thieves were hanged in the Old West; what was in store for cat rustlers? How would I explain this to the kids? Why hadn't I tried harder to find the rightful owner?

But then the woman's mouth cracked into a sly smile, and she said, "It's okay. Don't look so worried. Squeaky needed a good home. My name is Bonnie; what's yours?"

"Lucy," I responded with obvious relief at my good fortune and stretched out my hand to grasp hers. As it turned out, our Pancake, aka Squeaky, had started his odyssey on a suburban street in a box where children were trying to get rid of unwanted kittens. A family with two youngsters adopted him, but soon learned they were moving out of state and couldn't take the one-year-old cat with them. Bonnie, being the animal lover that she was, had three cats already, but she took Squeaky from the family rather than see him go to the shelter.

"But Squeaky never really liked it here," Bonnie explained. "He doesn't get along so well with the other cats, and he misses the children. You've done me a great favor."

Relieved that I wouldn't have to face a lynch mob after all, I invited Bonnie to come over and visit Pancake anytime she wanted, though that invitation proved to be unnecessary. She told me Squeaky had been making frequent visits back to her home all along. The clever cat was like a seasoned politician. He had been given away twice and then, like an emancipated teenager, decided to leave his third adoptive home for us, his fourth. But in his little cat brain he must have calculated that it would be good to leave all his options open and keep a paw and a food bowl in both places. This feline knew how to work his admiring public. If Bonnie's crew had better chow than we did some days, why not go over there to dine?

Squeaky, whom we now addressed by his real name instead of Pancake, was nothing if not a gourmet. In true regal fashion he let us know that only the finest, most expensive brands of kitty cuisine would suffice. We, his humble servants, of course yielded to his wishes. His favorite holiday was always Thanksgiving, a day on which we could hardly restrain the euphoric cat from crawling into the oven after the turkey and later into the refrigerator for the leftovers. Squeaky provided us with unlimited hours of comic relief.

That day in Bonnie's driveway marked the beginning of a long and dear friendship. Our mutual love of Squeaky kept us close even after Bonnie moved away. For many years, until Bonnie died, a Christmas card arrived in my mailbox each December with a handwritten note asking, "How's our cat?"

Though I had lived with cats before, I'd never had one that brought as much joy to my life as Squeaky did. He lived to be fourteen years old. Even after the children left home, Squeaky remained a constant in my life. With the passage of time he transformed from a playful cat into an omniscient old soul. When I needed comfort, he sensed it and would crawl onto my lap, purring and snuggling as if to say, "Everything will be fine." When he grew old and sick, I returned the love he had so unselfishly given our family. To this day whenever I eat pancakes, I can't help smiling as I think of that remarkable little creature sitting under the mulberry tree, plotting his next adoption.

Casey, My Little Cartoon Cat

By Rick Capone

Kittens are notoriously curious creatures, and my orange tabby, Casey, was no exception. If there was something that you didn't want him to get into, he'd find a way. No object was beyond his reach. No opening too small. If he was determined, nothing was going to stop him.

When Casey first came into my life, a number of things in my apartment caught his attention, but one thing captivated him beyond all else. The object of his heart's desire? The toilet.

Since the first day I brought him home, he was dying to know what was under the lid on the toilet seat. Every time we walked into the bathroom, he'd jump up there to check it out. He'd paw at the edge of the seat and try to pull the lid up, to no avail. He must have believed there was some great treasure underneath, because if I ever even hinted at lifting the lid, he was there instantly, ready to investigate. And when I flushed the toilet and closed the lid—which I always made sure to do—he'd climb up to see what all the noise was about.

One night I was getting ready for bed at about 2:00 AM. I was standing there with the toothbrush in my mouth and happened to look into the mirror just as Casey's head popped around the corner of the bathroom door. I saw his ears suddenly perk up and his eyes open really wide. What had caught his attention this time? Then I saw it—oh no! I'd left the toilet seat up!

Before I could even think about moving the few inches to close the lid, it was too late. Casey was airborne—he performed a perfect swan dive and went in headfirst. *Ker-splash!*

Now, a normal cat might have realized that it wasn't all that deep and just stood up and gotten out of there. But Casey was not a normal kitten. No sirree. My buddy Casey was the original hyperactive, panic-stricken, cartoon cat.

Instead of getting out easily, he went into freak-out mode, which consisted of flopping around like a fish, doing forward somersaults, twisting and turning in every direction, and then flipping over on his back, folding himself in half, and sinking to the bottom of the bowl. Once there, he twisted around, got his paws set on the solid surface, and then catapulted himself straight up out of the toilet. Then—while still airborne, mind you—he began a frantic running motion so that, as soon as he hit the ground, he had complete forward momentum. And believe me, once he hit the floor, he was gone in an instant—*zoom!*

Out the bathroom door and down the hall he ran, heading straight for, of course—the bed. Totally soaked, from the point of his nose to the tip of his tail, he looked like a scrawny little weasel. Up on the bed he jumped and then began shaking himself and rubbing himself all over the sheets, pillows, and blankets in a frantic attempt to remove every bit of water from his body.

There was never any threat of him getting hurt, as all this had happened in seconds. As I'd watched it unfold, I'd been laughing hysterically, almost to the point of rolling on the floor—until he jumped onto the bed. That wasn't funny, at least to me. Now I'd have to remake the bed and do extra laundry, two of my least favorite chores.

I grabbed a towel and headed for him as he was flip-flopping on the bed. That's when the real fun began: the chase. He saw me with the towel and in an instant was off and running again.

Now my apartment wasn't all that big, only five hundred square feet or so, but I'd swear we ran at least a mile. It was the classic chase scene. Casey went around the chair, under the chair, over the chair, under the table, up onto the couch, across the couch, under the desk, up onto the desk chair, up onto the desk, across the desk, down onto the table next to the desk, over the TV stand, across the living room floor—with me not far behind. Finally, he went into the kitchen.

Now I have him! I thought. *Cornered in the kitchen. Heh, heh, heh. Only one way in and one way out.*

Yeah, right.

We looked each other in the eye, and I slowly began to advance.

"Easy, little buddy. I just want to dry you off and make you feel better," I said.

I bent over to pick him up with the towel when, *zoom*, he was between my legs and gone. And so the chase continued, until finally he headed back for the bedroom where he went straight for, of course—the bed. *Ker-thump*, he landed on the bed and began a new session of flip-flopping.

This time, though, he was so busy flip-flopping that he forgot all about me. So I finally caught him.

I wrapped him up in the towel and gently dried him off a little, but he was still soaked. By now it was 2:30 in the morning, and I wanted to get some sleep, but first I had to get this kitten dried off somehow. Then I had an idea. *Pop!* I could almost see the requisite lightbulb appear over my head.

I know! I thought. *I'll use the blow-dryer.*

There's only one thing I can say about that brainstorm of mine . . . BIG mistake!

As soon as I turned the blow-dryer on, Casey's hair stood on end, and his claws dug into my arm to the bone.

I turned the dryer off and, claw by claw, undid his grip on me. I stroked him and let him settle down for a few minutes, then turned the dryer on to a gentler setting and aimed it at him from a distance. It took a while, but finally he was dry.

Needless to say, we both slept well that night—after I remade the bed.

Next morning when I woke up, guess where I found him? You got it! On top of the toilet, scratching away, trying to get underneath. With all he had been through just a few hours earlier, you'd think he'd have learned something. But then again, maybe it was as entertaining for him as it had been for me. Whenever I replay those scenes in my head, they're still just as funny as anything I ever saw on Saturday morning TV.

Feline Mayhem, Mischief, and Mystery

The Formative Years of Mikey the Carnival Cat

By Judy Merritt

He came to me as a tiny puff of fur running with all of his might across the park at Moose Lake, where the carnival that I worked for was set up for a Fourth of July celebration. Unbeknownst to me, he stopped underneath my food stock truck, which looked like a U-Haul, except painted blue with a red stripe along each side.

The inside was lined with wide shelves that held supplies for the two food wagons that I was in charge of: boxes of funnel cake, mini-donut, and corndog mix, enough sacks of sugar and cans of Flossine to make thousands of bags of cotton candy, plus a freezer full of hot dogs and cheese curds.

Against the back wall was a built-in bunk about the same width as the shelves. That's where I slept. The truck was my "livvy," a carnival term for a home on the road. It became Mikey's livvy, too.

I named Mikey after the carnival owner who had picked him up from his hiding place beneath the ramp and called me from the truck. I was rearranging stock to make room on the shelves for a big order for the holiday weekend.

"Hey, how's it goin'?" I said from the top of the ramp as my eyes adjusted to the bright sunlight. Then I saw the kitten sitting in the palm of his hand.

"I think he belongs to you," he said.

"Me?" I asked, taking the furry, strawberry-blond kitten with sweet blue eyes from Mike's outstretched hand.

"He came running across the park and stopped right here," Mike said. "I think he was waiting for you to find him."

Workers weren't normally allowed to have pets at the carnival, so I was thrilled. It often gets lonely on the road. That changed when Mikey ran headlong into my life.

He was beautiful and silky, and his fur glistened with copper highlights in the sunlight. At night he would curl up between my neck and shoulder and purr me to sleep. He loved to play pounce with my fingers and always made me laugh with his kitten antics, no matter how tired I was.

But his favorite game was hide-and-seek: he was always hiding, and I was always seeking. He would hide among the stock, piled high and deep on the shelves. I would call and call and search as best I could, but no Mikey. Just when I thought he was lost and gone forever, he would poke his head out from behind a #10 can of catsup or emerge from a box of napkins with a funny little "ha-ha" look on his face. Or he would stretch and yawn like he didn't have a care in the world.

We worked long days into the night, and I hated to leave Mikey in the livvy by himself, so I bought him a collar and a leash and walked him everywhere I went. I couldn't take the chance of not knowing where he was when it was time to pack up the carnival and head to the next town, which we did every Sunday.

When I was working on the midway, I would tie his leash to one of the games or the hitch on the back of a food wagon, depending on where I was stationed. Inevitably, every kid that walked by had to pet him and "ooh" and "aah" over how soft and cute he was. By the end of an afternoon of nonstop petting, Mikey would be literally vibrating from overstimulation. I would have to put him back into our livvy just so he could have some quiet time.

When he got a bit bigger, I'd tie his leash to a mop bucket. This gave him more freedom of movement but kept him reined in so I could find him when it was time to go. He was a sight to see, pouncing after grasshoppers with a bucket bouncing along behind him.

He brought smiles to the road-hardened faces of the ride jockeys, and every game operator wanted him nearby to draw people in to play their games. And they all kept an eye on Mikey to make sure we didn't lose him on the road.

We made it to winter quarters in Arkansas with Mikey still in tow. I stayed there for a while, helping to close down the show. Mikey didn't have to be on his leash in the fenced-in yard, and he was right at home, climbing about the girders and arms of the carnival rides that were all folded and tucked away until the next season.

When we were finished, Mikey and I headed cross-country to California to visit my brother Bob. Of course, everyone had to stop to pet him at every rest stop along the way. People were always amazed that Mikey walked on a leash like a dog. He was quite the hit when we stopped in Sedona, Arizona, and hiked along the red rocks with all the people looking for portals to higher consciousness.

At my brother's, Mikey must have been missing all his friends and the constant excitement of his carnival life. He slipped out of the house one day and disappeared. Though we combed the neighborhood looking for him, we came back empty-handed. But we were lucky. He ended up at the animal shelter, where they very nicely put a microchip in him before they gave him back to me for a fee.

My brother liked to take Mikey outside when he worked in his postage stamp–sized gardens. Mikey would follow him around like a puppy and play hide-and-seek in the tomato plants and in the rafters of the garden shed. A few times he climbed up onto the roof and explored the solar panels, thinking perhaps this was a new kind of carnival ride. Bob always had to keep a watchful eye on him to make sure he didn't start tagging along behind people walking by. Bob said he met more of his neighbors with Mikey in the yard than he had in the whole ten years he had lived there. By the time we headed back to my home in northern Minnesota, Mikey had really grown on my brother; Bob's favorite nickname for him was "If I Only Had a Brain."

I couldn't drive from California to Minnesota without stopping in the Black Hills. I had spent many years there wandering about the trails and had some favorite places I wanted to revisit. One was a spot the locals call Hippie Hole where a forty-foot waterfall crashes into rainbow mists. It's in the middle of nowhere, only accessible by a footpath at the end of an obscure and unmarked forest road.

Miraculously, I found the footpath and dutifully put Mikey's leash on him. We were about fifty yards into the trail, winding our way through rocks and tree-lined cliffs, when the quiet of the wilderness suddenly got even quieter. I had the feeling I was being watched. Mikey and I stopped at the same time and looked around. Mikey stiffened and I followed his gaze. A mountain goat was staring at us from a ledge not more than twenty-five feet away. He was so close I could have counted the growth rings on his thick, curved horns.

For a long moment, the three of us just stood there, looking at each other. Then, all of a sudden, the goat snorted. Mikey shot straight up into the air, bolted, and disappeared, collar, leash, microchip, and all. I searched behind every rock and tree—and there were a million of them—calling and calling, but no Mikey.

This was no time to play hide-and-seek. Mikey was lost in eighty thousand acres of wilderness, and it was almost dark. I was frantic. No little chip was going to help me find him now. I began to think I would never see him again.

When it became too dark to see, I gave up my search and went into town. I bought some hot dogs and matches, figuring I'd cook the hot dogs over a fire, and Mikey would smell them and come out for a bite to eat. He had to be hungry. That is, if he hadn't strangled himself on the rocks with his leash.

Worried sick, I drove back down to the trail. And there he was, waiting for me at the trailhead, looking as though he couldn't figure out why it had taken me so long to find him. I sometimes wonder if Mikey was playing pounce with that goat on the rocky cliffs while they left me behind to worry.

Our traveling days are behind us for now. We live in a small village in northern Minnesota (population 362) at the end of a dead-end street with a three-acre forest, where Mikey climbs trees instead of the folded arms of the Ferris wheel. He still loves to chase after grasshoppers and play hide-and-seek among the trees.

But every so often I catch Mikey staring off into space with a faraway look in his eyes, and I wonder if he's missing our adventures on the road.

Meows, Medicine, and Mishaps

By Amy Mullis

Pippin, my beautiful ball of orange fur, was sick, grumpy, and decidedly out of sorts. When she neglected her job as shift supervisor while the dog ate breakfast, I knew it was time for medical assistance. Playing overseer to ninety-five pounds' worth of German shepherd was her favorite pastime.

"Feline infectious anemia," the vet said, passing me pamphlets bearing diagrams of squiggly lines. I couldn't imagine my spunky girl the object of pamphlet-worthy discussion. Seeing documentation was frightening as well as comforting.

"Luckily," the vet purred, "we can treat this disease with tetracycline." Later, when I discovered Pippin would rather name the dog Queen for a Day than take her medicine, those words would echo through my nightmares.

But for now, I was ecstatic that Pippin would be cured. I left the vet's office with grand goals and good intentions, innocently clutching a bottle of tetracycline (man can create kitty litter that freshens with every step, but can't produce tetracycline in catnip mouse form), a needleless syringe for oral administration of the medication, and a despondent ball of fur. Cooing motivational speeches, I settled the kitty carrier in the car. The kitty inside glared at me through the metal bars and plotted ways to settle the score.

Once home, I pondered the situation and decided to take the honest, straightforward route. Taking up a syringe of sludgy liquid, I carefully explained the circumstances, Mama to kitty, stressing the importance of taking the medicine if she ever wanted to feel up to terrorizing the dog again. Pippin greeted this information with a cynical stare. I cooed, wheedled, and cajoled. She yawned, flicked one ear, and washed between her toes. All the while, gooey brown medicine oozed from the syringe, between my fingers, and down my arm, bonding my elbow to the kitchen floor.

Drastic measures were in order. I decided to try bribery. Perched on reddened knees on the kitchen floor, I had a panoramic view of all the places my broom had missed, including a disturbing view of the dust bunnies dancing under the refrigerator.

"Here, Sweetie," I sang, waving a tempting morsel of sautéed chicken with one hand, while proffering the sticky syringe with the other. Sweetie eyed the tidbit like it was a hair ball, presented me with her back, and licked her tail.

Time for action. I took a deep breath and lunged forward, accidentally depressing the syringe and sending a stream of brown goo across the room, where it splashed against the refrigerator and slid toward the floor, obscuring several of the offending dust bunnies from view and coating the rest in brown gravy. Kitty Dearest took up a defensive position across the hall under the bed, the feline equivalent of hanging a Do Not Disturb sign around her neck and activating an electric fence across the bedroom doorway.

After some minor injuries, and frantic telephone calls to the vet for advice, I found that by placing Pippin's back to the wall on the kitchen counter, I could cradle her body with my left arm, operate her jaws with my left hand, and administer the medication in small amounts through the syringe with my right hand.

Chain-saw jugglers should have a method that works this well. With lots of practice and more than one trip to the drugstore for sterile bandages and antibiotic cream, I successfully directed the majority of the medicine into the cat, leaving minimal traces on household furnishings and inhabitants. Of course, there are still stains on the wallpaper that I would rather not discuss. My first experience with administering liquid medicine to the kitty may not have been the Mama-to-puffball bonding experience I had hoped for, but thanks to good advice and guidance from my veterinarian, it was a successful endeavor. Through trial and error I eventually learned to give oral medication, a talent that, although not a big draw at parties, has come in quite handy over the years.

Miraculously, Pippin ended her tetracycline days with no outward signs of malicious thoughts or long-lasting resentment toward me for the atrocities that I inflicted on her feline pride in the interests of good health. She rebounded from her illness with enough energy to supervise the dog, doze away the days in the sunny living room window, and cavort in the kitchen with a fresh team of dust bunnies.

Time has healed the scratches and lightened the scars, but I will never again look at a sticky bottle of tetracycline and ten pounds of orange fluff without a trip down the memory lane that leads to Scar Wars. Pippin did make sure to get revenge. Not long after her recovery, I found her sprawled coyly on the kitchen floor, chewing holes in the syringe and smiling to herself.

Shotsie, Career Cat

By *Judi Moreo*

I came home from work one day and was startled to find a dish towel upstairs on the bathroom floor next to the laundry hamper. My first thought was that perhaps someone had broken into my home. I live alone and I don't usually bring dish towels up to the laundry hamper. I checked the house thoroughly and was relieved to see that nothing else had been disturbed. This was very strange . . . how could that dish towel have gotten there?

A few days later, I came home to find a sweater in the same spot. I knew I had left that sweater downstairs, but there it was, on the floor next to the hamper. What was going on? I was beginning to wonder if I had ghosts. Perhaps there was such a thing after all.

For the next few months, I continued to discover that anything I left out of place ended up next to the hamper in the bathroom. Maybe I had a ghost who was once a housekeeper! Whatever it was, it apparently had quite a need to have everything in its place.

Then one morning I woke up with a terrible cold and decided to stay in bed for the day. I hadn't missed a day of work in ages, but I really couldn't imagine going in feeling so poorly. About midmorning I was awakened by my cat, a Burmese named Shotsie, as she jumped up on the bed with a muffled cry. Opening my eyes with an effort, I saw that she had something in her mouth. It was the corner of a plaid wool throw that I had left downstairs in the living room. She pulled it up onto the bed where it usually is, then snuggled down in the covers to keep me company for the day.

That's how I discovered that Shotsie was the "mystery housekeeper." If anything is left out of place anywhere in the house, whether a jacket, blanket, towel, or whatever, she brings it upstairs and puts it either next to the hamper or under the bed. I marveled at her talent, one I had never heard of in a cat.

A few weeks later, a friend's daughter came to live with me for a while. Jennifer was not exactly neat. She left her clothing and belongings all over the house, and most of the time her room looked like it had been hit by a cyclone. Though I often reminded her to keep her things picked up, she sometimes forgot and dropped her clothes where she took them off: socks by the couch, sweatshirts in the hall, pajamas in the bathroom, and so on. But I soon realized that if I ignored them, she would eventually pick them up.

One day when only the two of us were at home, I heard Jennifer talking to someone in her room. I couldn't imagine who it was. As I walked down the hall, I could hear Jennifer insisting that her things be left alone. When I reached her doorway, I saw Shotsie in the middle of the room with the sleeve of a T-shirt in her mouth. Jennifer and I watched as she ran down the hall, dragging the shirt, and put it under my bed. Kneeling down to look, I found quite a stash of Jennifer's clothing. It was

Shotsie who had been picking up after her!

I had the idea that if Shotsie had a playmate to keep her occupied, she might not feel the need to be such a fanatical housekeeper. So I got another Burmese kitten. This little guy was a champagne Burmese and quite light in color, so I named him Brut. As soon as I brought him home, Shotsie took total responsibility for his upbringing. She taught Brut where the cat box was and where the food was kept. She also taught him that he shouldn't scratch the furniture. Each time he'd lift a paw to scratch the couch or chairs, she'd give him a swat.

I bought Brut a few small stuffed toys to play with, and before long I noticed that he and Shotsie were carrying the toys, one by one, from his toy box upstairs to the food bowl downstairs. Shotsie was teaching him to feed his "babies"! And so it began. Every morning the toys go downstairs to the food bowl, and when Shotsie decides they've had their fill, she and Brut bring them back upstairs to the toy box, one at a time. The more toys they get, the more work they do each day. Every morning, each little stuffed chicken, duck, turkey, cat, and dog goes down to the food bowl, and every afternoon they come back upstairs.

Now that she has Brut trained to feed the babies, Shotsie has taken an interest in a new profession. My marketing manager, Charlotte, recently started to work out of my home, and Shotsie has appointed herself Charlotte's helper. Each time Charlotte prints a document, Shotsie immediately jumps up on the table next to the printer and makes sure the paper comes out of the machine properly. Each time she hears the paper shredder start, she runs to check out what's getting shredded.

A lot of people will tell you that it's obvious their pets have careers. Some dogs have found steady employment digging holes in the yard. Others are major-league fetchers. The majority of cats think it's their job to give their owners someone to wait on hand and foot. My little Shotsie works really hard around the house. She's not only the best housekeeper and cat trainer I've ever had, she's also an administrative assistant. If only we could teach her to type!

Wild Cat, I Think You Love Me

By Janet Vormittag

Wild Cat bounced off the walls of the exam room in a desperate search for an escape. He leaped up onto a shelf that was packed with supplies. His added weight pulled the anchors from the drywall, and the shelf, along with its collection of boxes and bottles and Wild Cat, came crashing to the floor.

The fall didn't slow Wild Cat down one bit. He ping-ponged in circles around me and the veterinarian technician who was trying to catch him. She hadn't listened when I said the brown tabby was wild. When she had opened the cage, planning to reach in and grab him, Wild Cat had slid past her before she knew he was moving.

Wild Cat's story began a few months earlier. He appeared out of nowhere, as cats sometimes do, and moved into my barn, joining at least four other strays that had taken up residence in the same manner. I already had a number of cats living in my house with me, so bringing these new cats inside wasn't an option. I spayed or neutered them, and then fed them regularly, but that was all I could do for them.

Wild Cat, though a latecomer, assumed he was sole proprietor.

The quiet of the country erupted with fights as the barn cats tried to defend their turf. It wasn't long before I was taking Mama Cat and Buddy to the vet to have infected wounds tended.

Both cats needed antibiotics. I took them home, confined them to the basement, and tended their injuries twice daily. The house cats were kept upstairs.

Back in the barn, Wild Cat ruled. Boots no longer came around, and Rocky hid in the woods. That's when I borrowed a live trap. I set it only during the day, not wanting to catch any nocturnal skunks, raccoons, or possums. On day two, Wild Cat was mine.

"What a pretty kitty," I said as I approached the trap. He lunged and spat at me. "Let's hope the surgery takes away a little of your aggression." I'd already made the appointment to have the tabby neutered.

The technician was finally successful in catching Wild Cat. "Come back tomorrow afternoon and he'll be ready to go home," she said. The next day, Wild Cat was quiet, but I knew it was only because of the drugs.

"It'll take a few weeks, maybe a couple of months, before the testosterone is out of his system," she said.

For two weeks I kept Wild Cat in a dog kennel in the garage. There was no befriending him. He hissed; he growled; he continued to lunge at me. "You're a handsome guy. I'm not going to hurt you," I'd say in a nonthreatening monotone.

He apparently didn't believe a word I said.

The day came when I realized I wasn't making any progress in taming him. I opened the garage door and watched him sniff the fresh air. I opened the kennel door and stepped back. It took him a few seconds to react. Then he was gone. He ran so fast I thought I'd never see him again.

After Mama Cat and Buddy healed, they went back to the barn. Life was peaceful once again—until the weather turned cold. Wild Cat returned and so did the fights. He discovered one of the heat lamps that hung from the barn rafters, and I knew he wasn't going anywhere.

Mama Cat disappeared, probably to another barn in the neighborhood with a friendlier group of felines, and I brought Buddy back into the house. This time I introduced him to the house cats. After sniffing butts, they were accepting.

"You can be a couch potato," I told him. He became a double coucher, snoozing on the sofa in my office during the day and napping on the couch in the living room in the evening.

I debated if I should unplug the last heat lamp and quit bringing food to the barn for Wild Cat, but I couldn't do it, despite the trouble he caused. My Appaloosa had died in September, and without a horse to tend to, I had no reason to go to the barn every day. Still, I couldn't desert the elusive tabby who always hid from me.

I soon discovered that if I didn't slam the house door when I headed for the barn, and I tiptoed across the snow-covered lawn, I could catch a glimpse of Wild Cat through a window as he basked in the warmth of the heat lamp. By the time I made my way around to the door, he would be gone.

"Wild Cat, I know you're here. I brought breakfast." I'd pour the dry food as loudly as I could into the bowl. I knew he was hiding in the hay. It took a few weeks before he would answer my sweet talk, and then it was with low, deep growls. Over the next few weeks the growls evolved into faint meows. Then came the day when his head popped up from behind a bale of hay.

"There you are. Come down here and eat." He'd dodge back into hiding until I was gone, but as time passed, he slowly revealed more of himself.

"Come down here, and I'll scratch your back." The bribe didn't work. He listened from his perch on top of the stack of hay. Soon he was rolling around on his back and rubbing his face against the corner of the bales. "You're going to be domesticated yet," I teased.

We stayed at that level for weeks, Wild Cat strutting, rolling around, and rubbing himself against the hay. I kept coaxing him to come closer. Finally he came close enough that I could hold out my hand to him. I thought he would sniff it. Instead he swatted and drew blood. From then on I wore heavy gloves when I came visiting.

The day I successfully touched his head, we both panicked. I pulled back and he ran. Within a week of the first touch, I could pet him, but only if he was on a certain bale of hay. It was his safety zone, his home plate.

It was midsummer when Wild Cat discovered the back deck and its sliding glass door where he could peer into the house. It became his summer home, and I began putting his meals there instead of hiking out to the barn. We soon became yard buddies.

The inside cats didn't appreciate the outside visitor. They growled and tried to attack through the glass, but Wild Cat ignored their intimidation tactics. I remember the first time I left the sliding glass door open, leaving only the screen to protect Wild Cat from the house gang. Both sides took a step back. There was sniffing, growling, and finally acceptance.

I realized Wild Cat was pleased with his summer digs when he started bringing me gifts of dead animals—mice, chipmunks, and moles—poor choices for this vegetarian cat lover. I removed them from the deck with my eyes mostly closed.

When summer eased into autumn and the mornings were tinged with frost, I started carrying Wild Cat's food to the barn again. He followed me to the barn and then followed me back to the house.

"Your breakfast is in the barn," I told him. I felt a tinge of guilt as he sat outside the sliding glass door watching our every move, but I wasn't going to take the chance that he'd hurt the other cats again.

"Go to the barn" became my mantra. Wild Cat ignored me. Then came an early snow in October. Big, fluffy flakes drifted from the sky and started to turn the outside world white. Wild Cat curled into a ball in the corner of the deck. I couldn't take it. I opened the slider and screen door.

"Wild Cat, do you want to be a house cat?"

It was the invitation he had been waiting for. He strutted into the house like it was something he did every day. As he inspected the layout, the inside cats trailed him, taking turns sniffing his butt. He ignored them. The summer of being separated only by a screen door made the transition easy.

Two months later, Wild Cat is attacking catnip toys, snoozing by the fireplace, and chasing and being chased in play with the younger generation of house cats. He sleeps on my bed and insists on cuddling close.

Wild Cat's trust in me has evolved into a trust of everyone. He greets all who come into the house, whether family, friend, or repairman.

"Not everyone is as nice to cats as I am," I warn him. He listens, but he doesn't seem to have a shred of fear or distrust left in him. He knows any friend of mine is a friend of his.

A pile of leaves can be an excuse for a good roll.

Cats are keen to changes in their environment. After all, you never know when a mouse might stroll along.

Indoor cats never leave their instincts at the door—a hunt's a hunt, even if the prey is a toy.

Work to do? Cats will always help—by watching.

Cats like to "get high" and survey the world from above.

You are falling
under my spell . . .

A handsome cat can make even old furniture look great.

Hmm, I can't decide—take a
nap or pounce on a bird?
I guess I'm "on the fence."

The White Cat

By Diane M. Ciarloni

I was strolling through a yard sale one Saturday when I was stopped in my tracks by a painting of a white cat. An invisible but incredibly strong cord seemed to curl from the picture and wrap itself around my wrist, and there was no way to resist its tug.

It was a large piece, two and a half feet by three feet, with a frame of light-colored wood and a single decorative mat. The framing was attractive, but it was the cat that stopped me. I couldn't walk past.

The cat was totally white, and the artist had composed its face and head entirely of triangles. The ears were keen, sharply tapered triangles, and the small, peach-colored nose was a tiny triangle inside the larger one of his face. Both sides of the face were somewhat fleshed out, transforming the hard-edged geometric into a softer heart shape. The white fur looked silky smooth and lay flat against the angular body.

Sitting just inside the edge of a wood, the cat was partially hidden by leaves, tree branches, and graceful stems of irises and tulips. His face and head were completely visible to the viewer, but his body appeared fragmented, like pieces of a jigsaw puzzle.

The overall effect was that of an unfinished mosaic. From one angle he seemed to need something to make him whole. Then, from another angle, he seemed totally self-contained. It was this air of unsolved mystery that created the white cat's fundamental intrigue for me. It was also what told me I absolutely must own this piece of ten-dollar "art."

And so the white cat went home with me. I hung him on a generous expanse of wall where I could have the luxury of studying him several times each day. Nearly a year passed, and though I loved the painting, whenever I met the unwavering gaze of those yellow-green eyes, a sense of incompleteness nagged at me.

One morning I walked out my office door into the backyard. It was early, and a slight mist hung from the trees in the wooded area behind my house. The previous fall I'd planted iris and daffodil bulbs in the grassy nooks along the edge of the woods in an attempt at what the gardening magazines call "naturalizing." I saw that the flowers were just beginning to open. The frilly petals of the irises were deep purple, tipped in lilac, a rich counterpoint to the bright yellow daffodils with their equally vivid orange centers. The woods were always peaceful, and staring into them was like "soul watching." There was a lulling, hypnotic effect combined with a sense of wonder at all the creatures that must be living within that world of trees and vines. I finally turned to go back into the house. From behind me I heard a rustle as something moved among the leaves.

It moved again, and then stopped.

What was it?

I turned slowly, not wanting to frighten whatever it was—and froze in sheer incredulity. I was looking directly into the eyes of the white cat who was captured in the print hanging in my living room. Everything was the same: his pure white fur, his triangular-shaped face and ears, even his position and pose. He was half sitting and half reclining, with his face and head turned toward me. Leaves, branches, and stems of irises and daffodils blocked out chunks of his body. Just like his two-dimensional counterpart, he appeared to be a work in progress.

An eerie feeling prickled along my spine. I once saw a movie in which a person in a painting suddenly came alive. Of course, I never believed such a thing could really happen, but if not, how did the white cat from the print make his way into my woods? Even the irises were the same!

I didn't attempt to approach him but just stood there, transfixed. Looking more closely, I saw that, unlike the cat in the painting, he was painfully thin. In fact, I had no idea how any creature could still be alive in that condition. Even from a distance, I could see the ugly knobs down his backbone. I knew exactly how they would feel under my fingers; I'd rescued enough animals in my time to recognize starvation when I saw it. His hip bones were sharply pointed, rising above the profile of his back. The cat hadn't moved, but lay watching me, alert and wary. I squatted down and tried calling, softly. "Hey, white kitty. Come, white cat." He still didn't move.

I went into the garage, fixed a bowl of dry food, and set it outside the garage door in a spot that I thought he might visit. That was all I could do.

The next morning his bowl was empty, and when I went into the garage to feed our two outside kitties, I heard a scurrying and saw a white streak shoot through the cat door. *So,* I thought, *he found his way into the garage. That's good.* Everyone must have respected one another's territory, since I'd heard no sounds of scuffling during the night. The white cat continued to make frequent visits to the garage, scarfing up whatever food the others might have left. Of course, I made sure I put out more than enough for everyone.

Now, eight months later, the white cat has changed dramatically. Most of the sharp angles are gone, and his face has assumed a pronounced heart shape. But like the cat in the painting, he still sits far enough into the woods that parts of his body seem to be locked forever from view behind leaves, branches, and iris stems. And he still doesn't come to me when I call him. I've always won over animals in the past, but not this time.

I don't know what the connection is between my two white cats, but I believe there is one. Though I may never hear the cat in the woods purr, or feel my own skin come into contact with the sleek smoothness of his fur, when I gaze at the cat in the print, I can't help but feel that something's changed. I'm no longer struck by that sense of incompleteness. His face . . . his eyes . . . seem more at peace with the world. It may sound ridiculous, but he almost seems happy—as if he's now whole.

The whole thing remains a mystery, but no matter. Today I've come to see that the difference between the real and the unreal can be a very, very thin line, and that there are times in life when it's far easier to touch and embrace a fantasy than to lay even the tip of one's finger on the reality. The white cat is proof.

Inseparable

By Bettina Kozlowski

The elderly man had collapsed in broad daylight in a Chicago park on a beautiful July afternoon. Someone had called an ambulance. When the paramedics arrived, they found a heavyset man lying on the ground, curled up on his side with his back to them. There was no one else around. Nearby were a battered pet carrier and a shiny black trash bag, the kind the homeless typically use to store their clothes. The paramedics could hear the man moaning and were glad he was conscious. Getting closer, they saw a sweet-faced, balding man who didn't smell of alcohol and whose shirt was faded, but clean.

"Can you tell us what happened?" asked one of them, as he bent over the patient.

"It's my knee," the man stammered. "I can't get up!"

Gently rolling the man onto his back, they saw that he was clutching a petite, brown and white cat in his arms. The cat, whose heart-shaped, white face was accented by a chestnut-colored mask, looked at the strangers with that unwavering, wide-eyed stare unique to cats, which can turn into a hiss or a purr at any second. She didn't meow or fidget and seemed surprisingly well fed for a pet who appeared to live on the streets with her human companion.

"This is my girl, Kelly!" the man said, gripping the cat more firmly. "I'm not going anywhere unless she comes with me."

The medics paused and looked at each other. They knew they were breaking the rules, but they loaded the man, who was still holding on to the cat as tightly as he could, onto a gurney and into the ambulance. The cat did not budge, clinging to him like a baby to its mother. As the ambulance pulled away from the curb with its siren wailing, the medics shook their heads and laughed good-naturedly. They'd never transported a man glued to a cat before.

～ ～

The caller ID panel on Marijon Binder's phone read "Swedish Covenant Hospital ER." The name filled Marijon with a familiar dread. Maybe something had happened to one of her elderly friends whose cats she fostered or to one of the seniors whose pets she and her volunteers fed and cared for when the seniors were no longer able to do so.

The voice on the other end said, "Marijon, my name is Karen, and I'm an emergency nurse at Swedish Covenant Hospital. I called you because I know you help people with pets. . . ." There was a pause. "We have a patient in the ER we need to examine, but he won't be separated from his cat. Can you please come and tell him you'll take care of her?"

It was the first time Marijon had been called to a hospital emergency room to pick up a cat. "I'll be right there," she answered. "Thanks for calling me."

Since I first became acquainted with Marijon and her unique charity organization, Touched by an Animal, I've never known her to say no to anyone in need of help. This has meant going out in freezing Chicago winters to rescue pregnant, homeless cats and their unborn kittens, or rushing to the homes of elderly people who've called, panicked, because social workers are about to transfer them to a nursing home, and they're afraid they'll never see their beloved cats again.

Marijon, a senior citizen herself, arrives at these homes before Animal Control can pick up the cat, and she takes the animal in, sometimes until its human companion is released from the nursing home in good health—sometimes for good. Marijon and her volunteers frequently bring the foster cats to visit their human companions in the nursing homes. She keeps these "fosters" in a shelter she founded single-handedly, where they mix with the cats she's rescued from abandonment or saved from the street. Her charity organization covers all costs for the care of the animals, so Marijon works tirelessly to raise funds to stay afloat,

That July afternoon, after she'd hung up the phone, Marijon immediately stuffed a pet carrier with blankets and cat toys and rushed to the hospital in her minivan.

At the hospital, Marijon found the man lying in a bed in an examination room with the cat resting on top of the sheets facing him. Her paws perfectly aligned on his chest, the cat looked like a dainty Sphinx, warning, "He's mine; don't hurt him." The cat turned her head toward Marijon, and her big, emerald eyes blinked curiously at the sweet-looking, elderly lady.

She learned that the man's name was Patrick. He was a jovial and kindhearted man of Irish heritage who had fallen on hard times a few months before his accident in the park. He'd lost his wife, his family, his job, and his home, but he swore he would not be separated from his cat, Kelly, his "fair Irish lass," as he called her.

Patrick told Marijon that he'd adopted four-year-old Kelly two years earlier from the Anti-Cruelty Society and taken her home on a bus. Every afternoon, Kelly would perch on the windowsill of his old apartment, waiting for him to return from work. As soon as she spotted him, she'd run to the door and greet him with her tail straight up in the air like an arrow. Evenings, they'd snuggle on the couch and watch TV together. In the summer, he would share his peach-flavored ice cream with her. Those were good days.

Now he said, "They want to phone Animal Control to come get her." His face was very pale. "I know they'll kill her tomorrow if I don't come for her. I won't let them take her!"

"They won't take her," Marijon said firmly, stroking Kelly's forehead, which the cat pressed against her palm. "I promise you, I will give her a good and safe foster home until you get well and can be with her again."

Finally, Patrick nodded and quietly allowed his cat to be taken from him, "Take good care of her," Patrick said softly, looking at Kelly cradled in Marijon's arms. "She's all I have."

I met Kelly and Patrick a year and a half later on a frigid Sunday afternoon in January. Tired of just supporting the shelter financially, I'd shown up at Marijon's house to become a "hands-on" volunteer. Looking around at all the free-roaming felines, my eye was caught by a petite, brown and white tabby with a heart-shaped face and big emerald eyes sitting erect on a windowsill, looking out at the barren trees in the winter sun. She seemed melancholy.

"That's Kelly," Marijon told me when I asked. "She hasn't seen her dad, Patrick, in nearly a month." Patrick had entrusted Kelly to Marijon permanently, after complications from a knee replacement surgery had forced him to move into a nursing home. Though Marijon took Kelly to see Patrick as often as she could, the needs of other people and their pets had suspended the visits that month.

Ten minutes later, I was driving down the city streets, Kelly meowing, clearly not pleased, in a carrier on the passenger seat of my car. Without knowing what to expect, I'd spontaneously volunteered to bring the cat to Patrick's retirement home, so they could spend some quality time together.

When I took Kelly out of her carrier and placed her in Patrick's arms, the cat leaned her body gently against Patrick's chest, placed her front paws against his left shoulder, and rested her face against his neck. It looked as though she were trying to whisper into Patrick's ear. They stayed in that position for nearly an hour, like two lovers hugging after a long separation.

Other people came up to Patrick, admiring Kelly and stroking her fur. Patrick smiled. For as long as he could be with her, he had eyes only for his precious cat. Time passed too quickly for us that afternoon. Saying good-bye to Kelly was difficult for Patrick. I, too, felt tears well up in my eyes at the thought of separating this man and his beloved cat. I promised to return with Kelly next week. Patrick beamed at me and nodded. "It sure is appreciated," he said, "She means everything to me."

On our way home, Kelly didn't meow once. I can't be sure, but I suspect that we both were thinking of Patrick.

Marijon is still looking for a retirement home that will allow Patrick and Kelly to be together. Her dream, she says, would be to establish her own retirement community, one in which seniors can live with their cats and dogs, sharing their lives with each other every day—the way that families do.

Must-Know Info

Must-Know Info
Picking Out the
Purr-fect Kitten or Cat

When the weather warms up, so does feline romance. That soon means kittens who need new homes are suddenly everywhere. But with so many to choose from, how can you decide which one fits with your personality and lifestyle?

Work with a reputable shelter or rescue group to make sure the kittens you're considering are in good health and have had the benefits of gentle handling by staff and volunteers. Even kittens born wild can usually be tamed, but they need to be exposed to people early to grasp the advantages of being a member of a human family.

Faced with so many kittens, many prospective adopters choose based on looks alone. Some favor tuxedo cats, others red tabbies. Unusual markings can get other kittens adopted, such as "mustaches" or mittens, perfect symmetrical markings, or pretty patches of rich, contrasting colors.

But personality counts, too, which is why when you're looking at choosing from a shelter full of healthy kittens, it's a good idea to look beyond the markings to consider the cat within.

The feline personality ranges from the love-everyone attention-seekers to cautious, cold-shoulder types. Remember that what you see in a kitten is a window into the personality of the cat that baby will become. Kittens are creatures of their genetics and of what they experience in the first ten weeks of life. Sadly, a terrified or unfriendly kitten does not offer the best possibility of becoming a loving family pet. So for most people, it's better to choose from among the more promising contenders.

Based on years of experience, we've "cat"-egorized kittens into five personality types, along with the kind of home each is best suited for.

The activity junkie. Look at that kitten go! These crazy kittens are in constant motion and will likely become cats who are also busy-busy. Choose one of these kittens and expect an explorer who's always on the go. If you like an entertaining companion, this is the kitten for you.

The me-now meower. Look at me! Pay attention to me! As cute as these kittens can be, remember that if you like a quiet house, you might consider another baby. Cats are nocturnal, and the noisy, demanding kitten can become a middle-of-the-night alarm-clock cat. Still, many people love a cat who communicates.

The big-league batter. Your finger? It's a kitten toy! These kittens will reach between the gaps in their shelter enclosures to grab your fingers. These lively youngsters will crave playtime with you and will use all the kitten toys you can offer. If you can't provide daily, regular play sessions with these tiny tigers, you may find these felines ambushing your feet.

The purr machine. Love and lap time are what these babies crave. Touch them or even look at them and their motors start instantly. As adults, they will be happiest when near you and not happy when left alone. This type is an excellent choice for the person who's home a lot and wants an easygoing lap cat.

The socialite. These friendly, take-it-all-in-stride youngsters are a good match for homes with children and other pets. The socialite eagerly approaches the front of the kennel to meet and greet you—tail is up, ears forward, looking for a finger to sniff. These kittens should mature into cats who aren't easily flustered by a busy household.

Of course, you don't have to adopt a kitten. Many lovely, well-mannered, and healthy cats end up in need of new homes through no fault of their own. For many people, an adult cat is a much better choice—"instant" cat, no dealing with kitten craziness

When you are considering adoption, there are ways to uncover a cat's personality, even in the first meeting. When you first greet a new cat, extend your index finger so it's pointing right in front of the cat's nose, but not touching. Watch to see if the cat pushes her nose out to touch your finger. The nose-touch greeting is based on normal cat-greeting procedures. Much like humans shake hands when meeting, cats touch noses in the feline equivalent of a handshake. If the cat pushes her nose out to touch your finger, or rubs her cheek on your finger, it's a good indication she is well socialized and friendly. If the cat cowers, hisses, or runs away, she is displaying antisocial behavior and may be an unfriendly cat.

Next, pick up the cat and watch her body language. If the cat's muscles are relaxed and her body is loose, you are probably holding a friendly cat. On the other hand, if the cat goes rigid in your arms or squirms to get away, the cat may not be as social.

Try playing with the cat. Playing with a kitten will not be a significant indicator of the cat's personality, because almost all kittens love to play. Yet, playfulness in an adult cat is significant in indicating a well-adjusted and socialized cat. Take a string or cat toy with you when cat shopping. The cat that swats at or tries to pounce on the toy may be more well adjusted than the cat that simply ignores or runs from the toy.

Instead of a thermometer, gauge the cat's purr-ometer. The general rule of thumb is that the faster and longer a cat purrs, the better. Start petting the cat and observe how long it takes before he starts purring. If the cat purrs within two seconds, it is a great indicator. Next, pick up the cat and pay attention to how long it takes before he purrs. Also pay attention to how long the cat keeps purring while you hold or pet him. If the cat purrs for most of the duration of your time, you are probably with a very friendly cat. On the other hand, if the cat does not purr, or only minutely lets out a purr, the cat may not be as friendly. Pet and hold other cats to observe their purring behavior in order to compare it to your cat. Comparing the cat's purring can help give you a good scale by which to measure the cat's purr-ometer.

The final step is passing the cat to another person, whether it is a family member or a person working in the shelter or store. Watching how the cat responds to another person will help you decide how well adjusted the cat would be if it was brought into your home, and also helps to show whether or not the cat will be sociable with your family members or guests in your home.

Susan Tripp and **Rolan Tripp, D.V.M.**, have followed their hearts into a career helping people develop better relationships with their pets. Their pioneering website, www.AnimalBehavior.net, focuses on this increasingly important aspect of veterinary practice. The Tripps write *On Good Behavior* for the Pet Connection syndicated newspaper feature. Dr. Tripp has lectured and made presentations on animal behavior around the world, and he is an affiliate professor of applied animal behavior at both Colorado State University and the University of Wisconsin. He is also the principal veterinary consultant to Petmate, one of the largest manufacturers of pet products in the world. With a background in teaching, writing, and speaking, Susan Tripp shares her husband's passion for developing kinder, gentler experiences for pets in veterinary practices and at home. The Tripps owned the La Mirada Animal Hospital (California) for ten years, during which time Susan helped to transform the practice by offering community seminars, a volunteer program, puppy kindergarten classes, day care, deluxe boarding, and gentle grooming.

Must-Know Info
Solving Litter Box
Problems

For outdoor cats, the world may be their privy, but when toilet choices for indoor cats become the houseplants, behind the armoire, under the bed, or on their owner's clothes, the bond between family and feline can be severely tested or even broken. Indoor cats become outdoor ones, or worse yet, end up in a shelter.

Cats don't urinate outside the litter box to spite their owners. Some cats who don't go to the bathroom where we'd like them to have a medical or metabolic problem. Others are terrified of bully cats; still others don't like to do their business in a box that smells like a standing-line-only carnival Porta-Potty on a hot summer day. Many homes have too few litter boxes, located in the wrong places, or filled with litter that cats don't really like.

But with some simple, surefire steps many cases of inappropriate elimination can be greatly diminished or eliminated. For tougher cases, a referral to a veterinary behaviorist or new medications may make the cat purr and the owner smile.

At referral veterinary practices, close to half of the feline problems are for inappropriate elimination—not using the litter box. It's also one of the primary causes of removal of the cat from the home. There are three main factors in getting a cat to use a litter box: access, cleanliness, and litter type.

The first step in dealing with a cat who isn't using the litter box is to make sure a medical issue isn't causing the problem. That means a complete examination with diagnostics to rule out infections or other illnesses that make getting to a box a problem.

The litter box should be located off of the sleeping area but on the perimeter of one of the core areas the cat spends time in, along one of its traveled routes, but not off somewhere dark, dingy, and remote. The box should be large enough so that a cat can enter easily, dig, and bury his feces.

Cleanliness—or lack thereof—will turn a cat away from a box pretty quickly. Scoop more than once a day; if possible, aim to scoop after every time the box is used. There are even self-cleaning litter boxes that clean after each use, which might be very effective if they do not frighten your cat. Clean once every week or two with mild soap and water. While you might want some scent on the box, you should replace the box if it harbors strong odors even after cleaning (plastic impregnated with urine).

What's in the box counts, too. Most cats prefer litters that are clay or clumping, materials cats can dig in and are easy to clean. Sometimes the cat doesn't care what kind of litter you use (they'll use them all), and in this case the owners can pick based on their preference (clumping, scented, etc.). One thing for sure, if the cat is successfully using his litter box, don't change the litter. If you're having trouble getting your cat to use the litter box, and you've already eliminated other possibilities (such as not enough litter boxes, boxes in inaccessible locations, boxes not kept clean enough, medical problems), then you can let your cats pick their own litter. Do preference testing by trying three or four different litters and depths, different litter box sizes and designs, and positioned in two or three different locations, but try to change one factor at a time so that once you are clear which litter is favored, you can then work on what would be the favored box design and then perhaps the location.

Litter box choice is highly variable. Determine what you and your cat prefer by testing with different box types and locations. Start with these guidelines: have enough boxes that your cats don't get into conflict. If your cats compete or block access to food, litter, sleeping places, or scratching posts, then be certain you have enough of each of these to avoid conflict. You may need to consider placing litter boxes in two different rooms. Start out with the largest size litter box you can afford and have room for, but be prepared to change types if it doesn't work out. As far as where to locate the litter box, make sure it is not too far away from the core area, especially for a new kitten (because she might not wander into the area where you have placed the box).

If you have multiple cats and soiling problems, add boxes and clean more frequently as your first solution. Then try adding at least one new location: Try to find a spot with easy access, good lighting, and away from the feeding area, with nothing that will scare the cat (avoid the laundry room with noisy washer, furnace room that may be too warm or the cat is scared of the blower, or bathroom where the cat cannot access his/her box when bathroom is in use by family members). Basically, you can't have too many boxes in the house, but you can definitely have too few.

Spraying is not the same as missing the box. A cat who's spraying is marking territory, backing up to an object while standing with tail erect, and shooting smell-impregnated urine on the object. If the cat is spraying, it is most likely under stress or marking because of new cats or new odors. If your cat is not neutered this should be your first step! If you can't reduce the conflict and resultant stress (for example, block off windows so the cat can't see other cats), you may need pheromones or drugs to reduce the problem.

A fair amount of scientific evidence exists showing that pheromone treatments improve urine marking. (Treatment doesn't eliminate it in all cases but usually reduces it.) The pheromone treatments are synthetic versions of the feline cheek gland pheromone that helps to calm cats, and that cats use when rubbing up against your walls and furniture. Only cats can detect this, not humans. When they rub their cheeks on something— the corner of the couch or your ankles—they do this to make their environment familiar (cheek gland marking) and to reduce stress. The absence of a familiar pheromone may cause a cat to mark; therefore, you can use pheromones before a cat enters a new house, room, or cage, and this will encourage him to eat and eliminate normally.

Gary Landsberg, D.V.M., is board-certified in veterinary behavior both in North America and in Europe. In addition to his general veterinary practice, Dr. Landsberg offers behavior consultation services at the North Toronto Animal Clinic. He is a frequent speaker on behavioral topics at veterinary conferences around the world and has coauthored a number of veterinary behavioral texts as well as a series of behavior brochures. Dr. Landsberg has also hosted his own TV and radio shows. He was awarded the American Animal Hospital Association award for his contributions to the field of companion animal behavior and is a past president of the American College of Veterinary Behaviorists. His website is www.northtorontovets.com.

Must-Know Info
Preventive
Healthcare Tips

Most veterinarians would say that cats are living longer lives today, and more advances have been made in the last twenty years in feline medicine than in any previous time. We know more about nutrition, kidney disease and lower urinary tract disease, infectious diseases, and senior cat health than we knew a generation ago. We have excellent vaccines available to prevent the diseases that kill kittens. We have much better treatments for common chronic diseases of middle-aged and senior cats, such as diabetes and hyperthyroidism.

⌁

The single most important investment in a cat's health is wellness care: regular examination by your veterinarian. In kittenhood, more frequent visits are required to test for common diseases, provide vaccinations against life-threatening diseases, and provide treatments for common problems such as parasites. Having a good start in life sets the foundation for the years to come.

In a cat's middle years, veterinarians can help prevent problems that come with obesity, the most common nutritional disease seen in cats, and detect other common diseases in this age-group before the cat becomes debilitated. In the senior years, a cat may once again need frequent veterinary visits to detect common problems such as hyperthyroidism and kidney disease. Most of these diseases have effective treatments, even cures, as long as we identify them early. A good example is hypertension (high blood pressure), which can cause blindness and even death in senior cats but is easily detected and treated by a veterinarian. Obesity is a huge problem for cats (no pun intended!). We believe that up to one-third of cats are either overweight or obese, with the highest rates seen in the middle years of a cat's life, when up to 45 percent of cats may be overweight. Many cat owners may not recognize when their cat is obese and may not be aware of the significant health risks. Risk factors for obesity in cats include being a neutered male, having an indoor, sedentary lifestyle, and being fed a palatable, high-calorie, readily available diet. Here's an interesting fact—a cat who lives in a home without a dog is at increased risk of obesity!

The most common health problems associated with obesity are diabetes, liver disease, lameness, and chronic skin conditions. Other diseases linked to obesity include dental disease, lower urinary tract disease, and cancer. In addition, overweight pets are at increased risk if they require anesthesia or surgery, their immune function is decreased, their mobility may be poor, and they have decreased exercise and heat tolerance.

Veterinarians can help pet owners determine exactly how much food to feed, when to feed it, and what kind of diet to provide. These recommendations are individualized for the cat and the home environment. You will need your veterinarian's help to design a safe and effective weight-loss plan for an obese cat. A treatment plan will include dietary management, exercise (play!), behavior modification (for the owner!), and education on the nutritional needs of cats. The goal is to lose fat but preserve lean body mass and avoid the potentially serious health consequences of weight loss that is too rapid. Overweight or obese cats should never be allowed to go on a hunger strike, as a serious liver disease may result.

Oral disease is another common health problem. About one-quarter of cats have dental tartar, and about 13 percent have gingivitis. Cats have a feline version of cavities that are especially painful. Loose teeth, infections, and even tumors may be found in the mouth as well. The consequences of oral disease are serious—pain can impair quality of life and cause behavior changes such as hiding, irritability, and aggression. A painful mouth may prevent a cat from eating, leading to poor body condition. Unrecognized dental problems can lead to infections in the jawbone and abscesses. It is even possible that infections in the mouth can eventually cause problems elsewhere in the body if they are left untreated. Your veterinarian will assess your cat's oral health at each visit, noting any problems and discussing treatments.

Maintaining your cat's vaccination status is also important. Vaccinations are no longer recommended on an annual basis, but rather given as needed by your cat's lifestyle and other considerations. New vaccine delivery technologies are coming to the market as well, such as transdermal vaccines, which are needleless and do not include the chemicals that cause inflammation. These and other new vaccine technologies will improve our ability to protect cats against deadly diseases, for it is true that if we stop vaccinating our cats, we will go back to the days when many cats died of totally preventable diseases, an unacceptable situation to anyone.

Don't forget parasite control. Many cats live an outdoor or indoor/outdoor lifestyle and will come into contact with various external parasites such as fleas and mites and internal parasites such as worms. It used to be thought that heartworm was a dog disease, but recent advances in our understanding of this disease show us that cats get heartworm, too. The difference is that in cats, heartworm causes lung disease instead of cardiovascular disease. In fact, many cats with heartworm have been misdiagnosed as having asthma.

Fleas are no respecter of boundaries and will readily hitch a ride indoors with another animal, or even on our own shoes and clothing. Mosquitoes carry heartworm larvae, and while indoor cats are at lower risk of heartworm, they still may become infected since we all know that mosquitoes are very good at getting inside our houses. Talk to your veterinarian about protecting your pet.

What you put in your cat's bowl is also important. With all the recent knowledge on the role of diet in feline health and how it can contribute to diseases such as diabetes and lower urinary tract disease, it is more important than ever to think carefully about what food to feed your cat. No longer can we pick one food and feed it "cradle to grave." We know that kittens require very digestible food that is high in protein and energy, middle-aged cats require food that is lower in carbohydrates to help prevent or treat obesity, and senior cats get diseases that may benefit from specific dietary therapies. So diet needs to be tailored to lifestyle and health status—and by diet, we mean water, too! Veterinarians are able to help a pet owner select the best choices for each pet.

Susan Little, D.V.M., a board-certified feline specialist, is the president of the Winn Feline Foundation (www.winnfelinehealth.org). She serves on the editorial advisory committee of *PETS Magazine* and is a consultant for the Veterinary Information Network. Dr. Little is a contributing author to several publications, including *The Cat Fanciers' Association Complete Cat Book* and the Royal Canin *Practical Guide to Cat Breeding*, as well as several veterinary journal articles. She is a peer reviewer for the *Journal of Feline Medicine and Surgery* and the *Canadian Veterinary Journal*. She is also an internationally known lecturer on feline medicine.

Must-Know Info
Recognizing, Treating, and Preventing Pain in Cats

"Pain is inevitable. Suffering is optional," says Christine Longaker of the human hospice movement. Animals feel pain just as humans do, and just as with humans, there are ways to ease the pain and keep the joy and mobility present.

It's particularly challenging for veterinarians and cat owners to recognize when a cat is in pain. Cats can't "talk" to us about their pain, and they are descended from predators. Predators who can't hunt become the hunted and end up as a stronger animal's dinner. Even in today's household, where the biggest threat the cat faces is not frequent enough openings of the treat drawer, cats often will hide pain or sickness from those around them. From an evolutionary perspective, it is not in a cat's best interest to demonstrate weakness.

Pain is a highly individualized experience. The big Maine coon cat may have a high threshold for discomfort, while the delicate Siamese can barely tolerate a broken nail. In cats, as among humans, pain is a highly individual experience. Subtle changes in a cat's interactions with the family may be a clue that pain is present. Be on the lookout for unexpected hiding, irritability, lack of appetite, or just plain weird(er) behavior.

Most pain falls into one of two categories—acute or chronic—and these need to be treated quite differently. Acute pain is most often encountered following surgery, trauma, or injury. If a procedure will hurt a human, it will hurt a cat to about the same degree. Pain is best prevented by delivering pain medication before the painful procedure is performed. Surgical pain prevention and management strategies can be tailored to match the anticipated discomfort. Chronic pain most commonly arises from degenerative joint disease (osteoarthritis), and it presents its own challenges, which can include loss of appetite and depression.

Never give your cat medicine out of your own medicine chest. Unfortunately, many of the lifesaving medications a person takes can be fatal for a cat. It is *never* appropriate to reach into your own pill vial to try to "fix a feline," even when you think he may be in pain. Instead, call your veterinarian or the nearest veterinary emergency clinic for the best advice.

Sometimes the best pain management doesn't even require medication. Nonprescription methods of managing pain are emerging as useful tools in the feline pain management tool kit. Acupuncture is well accepted by cats, as is physiotherapy—including exercise in an underwater treadmill! Nondrug options may be used with or without helpful pain management medications. Your veterinarian will tailor the program to meet your cat's needs.

Nutrition makes the world go 'round. High-quality food and nutritional supplements that are appropriate for your cat's stage of life can mean the difference between just living and thriving. Overweight cats are at greater risk for the pain of osteoarthritis, so optimum nutrition can be used to achieve ideal body condition, minimizing discomfort and maximizing mobility. Fit beats fat hands down!

Help aging arthritic cats with their vertical moves by managing your cat's "ecosystem." Cats enjoy jumping onto the window ledge to watch the birds outside, so help them do so with less effort. Carpeted kitty steps may be just the ticket to more comfortable ups and downs.

Raise food and water dishes to between elbows and shoulders. Cats with back pain appreciate not having to "bend over" to eat and drink. Food and water dishes at elbow height take a tremendous strain off the lower back, making a simple activity like dinner far more enjoyable.

Slippery surfaces can create a treacherous path through the house. Cats with osteoarthritis may be slightly unsteady on their feet, leading to spills on slick floors. Cover tile, hardwood, or vinyl floors with nonskid area rugs to prevent potentially disastrous falls. Prevent access to stairs if that becomes appropriate.

Finally, stick with the "pain program." Once your cat is engaged in a program to reduce pain, maximize mobility, and maintain comfort, do not make any changes without the input of your veterinarian. Because effective pain management plans are most successful when they involve a "multimodal" approach, all parts of the treatment plan work in synergy to create the best effect. Even a small change can throw the plan out of balance.

Robin Downing, D.V.M., is a pain management consultant and lectures internationally on the importance of preemptive pain management in the compassionate care of companion animals. She is the current president of the International Veterinary Academy of Animal Pain Management and is one of only five veterinarians in the world to hold the diplomate credential in the American Academy of Pain Management, the largest interdisciplinary pain management organization in human medicine. In 2001 the World Small Animal Association presented Dr. Downing the Excellence in Veterinary Healthcare Award (Small Animal Veterinarian of the Year). She is also an accomplished and popular writer on pet and veterinary issues. Dr. Downing serves as a trustee for the Morris Animal Foundation and is an affiliate faculty member at Colorado State University's College of Veterinary Medicine. She is also a certified veterinary acupuncturist and is a certified canine rehabilitation practitioner, having trained at the University of Tennessee College of Veterinary Medicine.

Must-Know Info
Anesthesia Is Safer
Than Ever for Pets

If there's one part of veterinary medicine that seems to worry the average cat owner most, it's anesthesia, especially when older pets are concerned.

The simplest definition of anesthesia is putting an animal into an unconscious state so the pet will be immobile and pain-free while a procedure is performed. Some cat owners consider anesthesia so high-risk that they refuse procedures that could have long-term benefits to a pet's health and comfort.

Although veterinary anesthesia can never be entirely risk-free, it's considerably safer and more comfortable now than ever. Veterinary medicine has benefited from the improved technology of human medicine: the same high-tech monitoring equipment is used to warn of problems with blood pressure, heart rhythm, and oxygenation. The safety margin is further increased with the addition of a qualified veterinary technician whose sole job is to watch those machines and to monitor the patient before, during, and after surgery.

While you might imagine veterinary anesthesia as a gas given through a mask over the animal's face, in fact the modern practice of preparing an animal for surgery is a no-size-fits-all combination of injectable medications (often combining anesthesia and pain-control agents), anesthesia-inducing gas, and pure oxygen, the latter two delivered through a breathing tube to maintain an animal's unconscious state.

In addition to constant monitoring by machines and trained technicians, the use of intravenous fluids during anesthesia is another safety measure. It gives the veterinarian instant access to a vein if there's an emergency. Intravenous fluids also help to prevent low blood pressure, which can be a common complication of most anesthetics.

Keeping an animal warm is another part of the safety protocols. A low body temperature delays anesthetic recovery and healing, and shivering increases oxygen consumption

A pre-anesthetic screening is also important when it comes to reducing risk. A thorough physical exam allows the veterinarian to determine any underlying problems and to recommend pre-anesthetic blood work. In a young pet, that could be just checking for anemia. An older pet may need a complete blood count, determining kidney and liver function, and making sure all organs are functioning normally. Any abnormalities can be addressed before surgery to further increase safety margins.

Even in older pets, health problems don't necessarily rule out procedures that require general anesthesia. You have to balance the risks with the benefits; your veterinarian can discuss these with you. How much pain is the animal in? Has your pet stopped eating because of a rotting tooth? Many older pets have problems that dramatically reduce their quality of life and leave them in constant pain. Fear of anesthesia on the part of the owner is no reason to leave an animal in misery.

Not all veterinarians use all the anesthetic safety protocols—sometimes because of the cost concerns of pet owners. It's important to have a frank discussion with your
veterinarian before your cat has surgery to understand how
your pet will be treated and why. With a knowledge of
what's available, you'll be able to make an informed decision when it comes to anesthesia and your pet.

Rachael Carpenter, D.V.M., is a clinical assistant professor of
anesthesia and pain management at the University of Illinois
College of Veterinary Medicine. She is also a consultant to the Veterinary Information Network. She has worked as an emergency and critical care veterinarian and did her internship at the prestigious Rood and
Riddle Equine Hospital in Lexington, Kentucky.

Mυsf-Kñ̤ọ̤ω lñ̈f̤o̤
Enrichment Activities
for Cats

Cats in the wild don't have walls or TV sets, and they don't hang out with other animals, especially other predators. They sharpen their claws on anything they want, mark their territory with pizzazz, and the world is their toilet. Even when first domesticated, they were working animals, mousers, ridding granaries and households of vermin.

Cats are not little people in fur coats; they are proud members of another species. Yet we shoehorn them into houses crowded with other cats, dogs, people, and lots of funny noises. Then we freak out when they exhibit behaviors not conducive to a harmonious human household, activities that are perfectly normal to them in the wild.

Today's cats are born retired. They've gone from mouser to moocher. And while retirement may sound good for a while, bored cats lacking from enrichment activities have weight issues and medical problems and may suffer physically and emotionally.

Environmental enrichment activities need to be our priority. When it is, cats will live happier, healthier, fuller lives.

To be at their best, cats need to have some basic needs met to help ensure their long-term health and welfare. When these needs are not met, cats may feel stressed, which can affect their health and behavior. Listed here are things an "ideal" house for cats might include. While some cats might not need all these features to get along, making homes more "cat-friendly" will ensure that owners and their cats enjoy each other's company for many years.

Provide a room or other space the cat can call his own, complete with food and water, a bed (a cat carrier with a soft pad inside is a good choice), a litter box, a scratching/climbing post, a window to look out of, and some toys.

Place food and the litter boxes away from appliances and air ducts that can come on unexpectedly, and locate them such that another animal (or human) cannot sneak up on the cat while he uses them. To keep them appealing to the cat, food and water should be kept fresh, and the litter box should be "scooped" every day.

Give cats something to scratch on to ensure that they can engage in this normal behavior without damaging furniture. Cats can easily be enticed to use scratching structures by placing them in places the cat likes, pairing with treats, feeding and playing near the structure, and praising profusely when the cat is seen using it.

Provide objects (a climbing tree or pine ladder) the cat can climb and look out of windows to provide more mental stimulation.

Cats seem to prefer feeling like they are "in control" of their surroundings and choosing the changes they want to make. When you make changes (food, litter, toys, etc.), offer them in a separate container next to the familiar one so that your cat can decide whether or not to change.

Be sure to see your veterinarian regularly. In addition to

providing preventive health care through regular checkups, they also can help you troubleshoot any "issues" before they become problems.

Understand that cats do not respond to force, and that they do respond to praise! Reprimands only work if the cat is "caught in the act." Punishment that follows an action by more than a few seconds won't stop the cat from doing it again, and may even cause him to become fearful of the owner or the surroundings. If a cat is caught making a mistake, it is better to create a distraction by making a loud noise or throwing something (not at the cat!) that will attract its attention, but not toward you.

Use treats for rewards and stress reduction, with "treat" meaning toy and play as well as food. The stress-reducing power of treats comes from their ability to stimulate mental and physical activity and positive interactions with the cat's owner. Cats also seem to have treat preferences; some prefer "birdlike," some "buglike," and some "mouselike" toys that mimic their natural prey. And some cats don't even like to play much; for them the owner's lap and maybe a gentle brushing are treats. The real key to stress reduction in cats and humans alike is to identify activities that make us feel better, and then doing them. The easiest way to learn what an individual cat prefers is to offer her alternatives and watch what she chooses. It's the same as we would do for a welcome houseguest from an exotic country who we couldn't talk to.

Tony Buffington, D.V.M., Ph.D., diplomate of the American College of Veterinary Nutrition, is a professor of veterinary clinical sciences at The Ohio State University Veterinary Hospital. Dr. Buffington is world-renowned for his expertise on pet nutrition and for his interest in the health of indoor cats. The Ohio State University College of Veterinary Medicine created the Indoor Cat Initiative (http://vet.osu.edu/indoorcat.htm) to enrich the lives of indoor cats, in the belief that indoor enrichment is as important to cats' welfare as an excellent diet and health care. Learn more about Dr. Buffington's work on his website at www.indoorcat.org.

Must-Know Info
Lost? . . . and
Found Quickly!

One of the biggest mistakes people make when pets go missing is underestimating the seriousness of the situation. When a pet gets out, the response should never be "wait and see." Your pet is about as capable of surviving on his own as a toddler is.

First on the to-do list: a "lost cat" sign.

Take a picture of your cat every year and include the most recent photograph on your sign.

You don't need to describe your cat from nose to tail. If you've lost a large, black cat, start with that: "Lost! Large, black cat!"

Also put the word "reward" in big, clear letters. Money can be a powerful motivation for someone who doesn't care otherwise, and it can be an incentive for someone to tell you who has your pet if it was stolen.

Leave out a piece of information that only the true finder would know, such as a distinguishing mark or the color of your cat's collar. Asking the finder to describe your pet will thwart scam artists who prey on people with lost pets, claiming to have the pet in order to collect a reward.

Make sure the sign can be easily read from the distance of a passerby walking or a car driving on the road. Include your phone number and area code—a cell phone number would be best (keep that phone with you and turned on).

A measure of "sappiness" should be your final touch: get people emotionally involved. Put "child is heartbroken" or "my best friend is missing." It really can help!

Print at least fifty signs on bright-colored paper and post them all around the area where your pet was lost. Post half of the signs so that they're facing the street where drivers can see them, and half facing the sidewalk, so pedestrians can read them. Poke a hole and thread a rubber band through the top of the flyer and hang copies from your neighbors' doorknobs.

Post in nearby places where the finder might go, such as veterinary offices, cat parks, pet supply stores, groomers, grocery stores, and the post office.

If your cat has been microchipped, contact the registry and let them know your cat is missing.

Tell your mail carrier that your pet is missing, too!

Next on your action list are these important tasks:

Place ads. Place a "lost cat" ad in local newspapers, and post it on Internet sites. Check the "found cat" ads in the same places.

Visit shelters. Visit every shelter within at least a fifty-mile radius of where your pet was lost. Since new pets are brought in daily, it's highly recommended that you go to the shelters every day. Shelter workers are busy, and they might not remember seeing your pet or recognize him from your verbal description, so visiting is better than calling. Ask to see the pets in the infirmary, as well as in the general runs, because your pet might have been injured.

While you're at the shelters, ask to check the listings of animals who didn't make it, such as those hit by cars. Hard as it is to know a pet was killed, it's harder to never know what happened.

Change your phone message. Record a message on all your phones (home, office, cell) that encourages people to leave a message. Suggestion: "If you're calling about my missing pet, I'm out looking for him right now. Please leave a message, and I'll call you as soon as I come in."

Enlist help. Ask friends, family, and neighbors to help you search by going door-to-door in your area. Ask neighbors to check their garages, toolsheds, and crawl spaces. Cats often slip into such spaces unnoticed and are trapped when doors are shut behind them.

Just as you shouldn't delay in trying to find your pet, you shouldn't give up too easily. People may tell you you're nuts to keep looking, but pets do turn up after weeks and even months of searching. Make sure your signs stay posted and keep visiting the shelters.

Liz Blackman, inspired by her own two rescued cats, Lita and Winchell, founded 1-800-HELP-4-PETS, an identification system that works like a nationwide 911 service for pets in any emergency—lost, home fire, car accident, natural disaster, and travel emergencies. Since 1996, 1-800-HELP-4-PETS has helped thousands of pets get help and get home. For more information, listings for lost and found pets, and advice on how to prevent loss or find a missing pet, visit these websites: www.help 4pets.com and www.thecenterforlostpets.com.

Must-Know Info
Shoot Your Cat—With a Camera, of Course!

Digital photography has changed everything for the casual photographer. Instead of wasting roll after roll of film—or not bothering to take pictures at all because of the trouble and expense of getting them developed—it's now possible to take hundreds of pictures, happy in the knowledge that if there are just one or two good ones out of every few dozen taken, nothing has been wasted except possibly your time.

Even better, photo-editing software has made it possible to salvage a marginal image. With a few clicks of the mouse, the out-of-frame, out-of-focus, or "just not right" images are jettisoned forever. A few clicks more and those images with potential are fixed up and made suitable for framing—a crop here, a "red eye" (the cat's eyes reflecting back in the image) changed to brown, the elimination of items cluttering up the background.

But the best pictures aren't made in a software program. They start with the knowledge of how to get great pictures at the first shutter click. Learn the basics and you'll end up with the memories that will last forever.

The best advice is to take lots and lots of pictures, but here are some more tips to get more from your picture-taking efforts:

Outside is best. Taking pictures outdoors gives your cat a more natural, healthy look, but many cats are indoor-only pets. If that's the case, use houseplants and windows to bring the outdoors in.

Use your flash. To bring out the detail in your cat's face if your cat is a solid, dark color, you'll need your flash. If you end up with red eye use photo-editing software (basic programs come free with many new cameras and computers) to fix the problem.

Get close. Sometimes you want, or need, to include your cat's environment to better tell the story, but in most cases, especially for portraits and personality shots, it's best to move in and fill the frame with your subject. The less "stuff" you have in the frame, the better. Get down—I don't mean dance—I mean get down, or up, whatever the case may be, to your cat's level. Get face-to-face and see the world from her point of view. Not only will this give you a better visual connection with your cat, but shooting from her level also helps to separate the background from the subject. For example, if you stand above and shoot down at your cat, the floor, which is only a few inches away, becomes the background. However, if you lie on the floor and shoot from your cat's eye level, the wall on the other side of the room becomes the background, giving you much better separation, which helps your cat stand out in the photo.

Watch your backgrounds. Think neutral—a plain wall, an uncluttered cabinet. And think contrast—light for a dark cat, dark for a light one. If your cat loves to curl up on his paisley cat bed, consider throwing down a solid-colored blanket before you shoot. You might be able to edit out a distracting background later, but it's easier to avoid it in the first place.

Be patient. If your cat does something cute and you miss it, don't despair. Chances are if you're patient and keep your camera ready, you'll catch the encore.

Get help. If your cat is relaxed around kids, enlist a child's help to get a cat's attention with a toy or treat. If you're lucky enough to have a multicat home, watch for times when they are engaging each other in play or grooming. And don't forget, there's nothing more adorable than cats snuggling up together for a catnap—with each other or their favorite human.

Be creative. If you want your cat to interact with a person or an object, do as the pros do: put a little butter on your hand and let the cat kiss it off, or rub a little catnip on a surface. Squeaky toys and laser pointers work well, too. If your cat will stay for a second or two, throw a toy in the direction you want him to look.

Have fun with software. The camera's just the first step to a great picture. Basic picture-editing software can do more than fix errors—it can turn your images into art! Play with colors, contrast, sharpness, and more, or use special effects such as "watercolorizing" to create something unique.

Keep taking pictures throughout your cat's life. Just as with children, people tend to take pictures of new kittens and then put the camera away. But your cat is always changing, and the image you may one day love the most is of your cat as a sweet senior.

When you've decided to share your new skills with the world and submit photos to magazines, newspapers, or books, first check the publisher's submission guidelines. Most publishers do not accept doctored photos (photo editors can tell!). This is where the pros stand out, but don't be discouraged—practice and cultivate your skill until you can achieve picture-perfect results with minimal help from technology.

So get out there with that new camera, whether it's a pint-sized point-and-shoot or a sophisticated digital SLR. You'll never find a subject more patient than your cat (well, we may be exaggerating!), especially if treats are involved for good behavior.

Troy Snow is a professional freelance photographer whose work has been widely published and appreciated. Along with a team from Best Friends Animal Society, he went to the Gulf Coast in the aftermath of Hurricane Katrina to help animals and people. The stories from that rescue effort are told by his stunning photos in the book *Not Left Behind: Rescuing the Pets of New Orleans*. Many of Snow's photos are on the Best Friends website (www.bestfriends.org), and you can see more of his work at www.troy snowphoto.com.

Must-Know Info
Cracking the Code of
Your Mysterious Feline

What seems crazy to a person is often perfectly normal to a cat. Once you understand why cats are as they are, you'll be better able to comprehend what seems to be mysterious behavior. Here's the mystery-solving behind many interesting feline conundrums:

Digging and burying around the food bowl, especially when fresh food is added. Many people believe the cat is attempting to keep things clean, covering the food in the same way they cover their urine and feces. This may be true if the food is not to the cat's liking. A more likely explanation is that the behavior represents an attempt to store the leftover provisions for safekeeping. Leopards, lynxes, pumas, bobcats, and other wild cats will cache their food when they make a big kill or when food is plentiful. They use grass, dead leaves, soil, and so on to safely conceal their food for future use. Feral domestic cats have been observed to do this on occasion as well. A house cat certainly doesn't need to save food, but don't bother telling this to the cat. This is an evolutionarily conserved behavior that's done by pure instinct.

Devotion to plastic bags. The exact cause of this behavior is speculative. Some have suggested that cats like the coolness of the plastic or the texture of the bag on their tongue, or maybe even the sound the plastic makes when it is being licked. One of the most accepted reasons, though, is that cats like plastic bags because rendered animal fat is used during the manufacture of these bags, and some cats can detect the smell and enjoy the taste. Petroleum products and gelatin that are used in plastic bag production are also seen as an enticing ingredient in the plastic bags. Gelatin is used in the manufacture of many items, including the emulsion used in photographs. Perhaps this explains why my own cat, Emma, enthusiastically licked clean a bunch of unattended photographs one afternoon.

"Wool" sucking. Some mistakenly classify wool-sucking as a form of "pica" (abnormal ingestive behavior, like eating plastic), but technically, it isn't. It is a compulsive, misdirected form of nursing behavior. In most cats, active nursing behavior occurs in the first seven or eight weeks of life, after which the mother cat deliberately rebuffs them so that the kittens learn to fend for themselves. Once kittens start to get used to solid food, the nursing instinct fades. If a kitten is weaned very early—when the nursing drive is still very strong—it may displace that craving to nurse onto items that look or feel like Mom. This can include their own fur, a littermate's fur, or some other fuzzy material, including wool. The younger the kitten is when it is weaned, the stronger the nursing drive, and the more persistent this extraneous suckling behavior may become. So-called Oriental breeds (such as the Siamese) seem especially prone to this behavior, perhaps suggesting a genetic component as well. In most cases, as kittens mature, the wool-sucking behavior diminishes; however, in stressful situations, those distant memories of this behavior may resurface as a way for the cat to comfort itself.

Catnip. Cat lovers marvel at the delight cats seem to get from smelling, nibbling on, and rolling in catnip. A behavioral response to catnip is found only in members of the feline family. Lions in particular demonstrate a rather spectacular response, and hunters have used catnip to lure bobcat and lynx. The typical catnip scenario for the domestic cat initially involves the offering of some catnip leaves, either fresh or dried. Cats will first smell and then lick or chew the stuff for a few minutes. Some cats show a "like, wow, man" response and just gaze off into space, as the extent of their reaction to the substance. Most responders progress to rubbing their cheeks and chin in the catnip source and act a little dizzy. The intense responders will rub their bodies on the ground while rolling from side to side, purring, growling, and perhaps leaping into the air. Reactions vary, although most cats experience both a relaxing and a stimulating effect. The complete response lasts for five to fifteen minutes, with a type of satiation developing so that a response cannot be evoked again for at least an hour or two. A large number of adult cats show zero or minimal response to the plant, and nearly all kittens under two months of age show no reaction to catnip and often actively avoid it. Males and females respond equally. Whether a cat is a responder or not is based on heredity; a recessive gene is involved, so that two cats from the same litter may have different responses to the plant.

Purring. Usually a sign of kitty contentment, purring is a voluntary behavior. Kittens and moms purr together when the family is nursing, and simply taking out the food container is enough to get many cats going. However, cats have also been known to purr when frightened or in pain, and experts believe that this behavior allows the cat to comfort himself. Others have suggested that it is a submissive behavior, a way to let other cats or predators know that they're not a threat. Since calming endorphins are released when a cat purrs, it makes sense that this behavior is as pleasurable to cats as it is to us.

Arnold Plotnick, D.V.M., a board-certified small animal internist and feline specialist, is the founder of Manhattan Cat Specialists (www.manhattancats.com), a full-service, feline-exclusive veterinary facility located on the Upper West Side of New York City. Manhattan Cat Specialists' goal is to continue to advance the cause of feline medicine.

What am I thinking?
Three guesses.

Nothing's as huggable
as a fuzzy cat.

Cats' ability to catch mice has always made them welcome on ships and around docks.

The orange-red color of many cats adds interest to their markings.

Cats love finding baskets and even boxes to snuggle in.

While kittens get the attention, an adult shelter cat can be a wonderful pet to adopt.

Cats can see well in conditions that would render humans virtually blind.

This is what you call
feline finger food.

Must-Know Info
What to Feed
Your Feline

Nutrition is one of the most important factors in a cat's overall health and longevity. Cats are not little dogs or tiny people in fur coats.

Compared to omnivores such as people or rats, cats have specific nutritional needs that reflect their evolution as carnivores. For example, cats cannot convert beta-carotene from plants into vitamin A, and they do not make vitamin D in the skin when exposed to sunlight. People can do both of these things. Also, cats need specific amino acids (arginine and taurine) in addition to the nine essential amino acids people need. Cats evolved on a high protein diet and have a high nitrogen requirement compared to other animals like dogs or people. While they can adapt to higher protein diets, they are not able to adapt to a low protein diet. There are other special needs, too, so it is important to feed your cat a diet specifically designed for cats.

The most common mistake is that many cat owners feed too much food (or too many treats) and allow their cats to become overweight. Less commonly, some owners give supplements in addition to a complete and balanced pet food. This can lead to excesses of some nutrients and is not recommended. Another mistake is to buy large bags of food or to stock up by buying more food than your cat will eat in four to six months. Purchase your cat's food at a store that sells a large volume of food and has a quick turnover of product. Food should not smell rancid, and it should be stored in a cool, dry place. Some diets are more prone to spoilage, such as those containing fish or fish oil, since the fats in these ingredients are fragile.

Most cats will do well eating any one of the various types of food. However, there are situations when food with higher moisture content is beneficial, such as for a cat that has had problems with urinary tract stones or crystals. For these cats, more dilute urine and more frequent urination can help prevent the stones or crystals from reoccurring. Other cats may have painful dental disease and can eat a canned diet more easily. By far, though, the most convenient and economical type of cat food is dry kibble. Some owners may choose to mix food types, such as feeding both dry and canned foods, and that is fine, too, as long as the individual cat is doing well.

There is a wide range of cat foods for every budget and to fill every possible market niche. There are no legal definitions for many marketing terms, including "premium" and "super-premium." These terms cannot be used to evaluate foods, since they are not descriptive of any standardized dietary or nutritional features. Likewise, celebrity endorsements and consumer testimonials are not recommended criteria for choosing foods. Instead, it's important to choose a food that has passed feeding tests for the life stage of the cat you are feeding (growth, maintenance, reproduction, or all stages), rather than one that has only been formulated by a computer. The label will tell you which method was used to establish the nutritional adequacy of the product.

Other factors may also influence your choice, such as the experience and reputation of the manufacturer. Be cautious of amazing claims and incredible statements. You should be able to easily contact the manufacturer to request documentation for any claims or to request further information (such as calorie content).

Cats develop fixed preferences for flavors and textures they are repeatedly exposed to, so it is a good idea to make sure your cat accepts a variety of kibble flavors and shapes as well as different canned foods (loaf type, chunks in gravy, etc.). Cats that have been fed a variety of foods are more likely to try something new when offered. The reputation for being finicky may be related to the fact that many cats, especially those that live indoors, have low energy requirements and do not need to eat much food to maintain their weight.

However, cats do have specific preferences for flavors that are different from other species. They don't show a bias for salt or sugar, for example. They also like the flavor of protein and amino acids and appreciate warmed foods. Many cats will also prefer foods with higher moisture content. Whenever a cat changes his normal behavior, and especially if he stops eating, contact your veterinarian right away.

Jennifer Larsen, D.V.M., Ph.D., is a board-certified veterinary nutritionist and clinical nutritionist with the Nutrition Support Service at the University of California Davis Veterinary Medical Teaching Hospital. She is also a consultant to the Veterinary Information Network and a member of the Scientific Advisory Board, Davis Veterinary Medical Consulting.

Must-Know Info
How to Redirect Your Cat's Inappropriate Scratching

There's no getting around it, cats are going to use their claws.

Clawing is a natural instinct for cats and is used to exercise and stretch, as well as a way to signify emotions and mark territory. Scratching is pleasurable for cats, as well. Some will also scratch when they're excited or on the prowl for prey, even if the "prey" is a toy. Many cats are even more apt to claw when around the scent of catnip, which also makes them "frisky" and more likely to scratch.

If your cat can't get outside to claw a tree, items in your home are the next best thing. Whether their claws dig into furniture, drapes, or carpet, cats don't tend to discriminate.

Before this talk about clawing has you sending your cat out the back door, take hope. Cats can be taught how to constructively claw by using behavior modification, which means using positive reinforcement to encourage them to use the scratching post and using negative reinforcement when they scratch on something they shouldn't.

Positive reinforcement is a very simple process, and you may only need to teach your cat a couple of times before he understands.

Most cats quickly figure out what scratching pads are for. If your cat is not sure, your whole family can scratch on it along with your cat to show him what to do—it's a great bonding exercise! Another effective method is to pull yarn or string across it; he'll start digging his claws into the scratching pad while chasing the yarn.

Scratching posts come in all shapes and sizes, from simple cardboard scratching pads to elaborate, expensive pieces of furniture. Certain coarse textiles on posts are attractive to cats, such as sisal, hemp, and loop fabrics. Cats don't care how big or how expensive a scratching post is; they just want any type of material that feels good to dig their claws into.

A cardboard scratching pad can be perfect for some cats, while others prefer ones made of sisal, a natural rough rope. Both of these are appropriate as they don't resemble any furnishings in your home. While many cats like carpeted scratching posts, they aren't recommended, since some will learn to associate scratching with carpets. You can't complain if your cat then scratches at your rug!

Locate your cats' scratching area in a quiet spot near where they sleep (most scratching is done right after they wake up) and make sure the scratching post doesn't move when they use it. Cats like to either get on top of the scratching pad if it's on the floor or bear weight against it if it's vertical. This means scratching pads hanging on a doorknob probably won't get much use.

What do you do if your cat's idea of a scratching post is your satin bedspread? The best form of negative reinforcement is to use a little water pistol or a spray bottle adjusted to a stream. When your cat scratches something he's not supposed to, spray him with some water. After you spray him, look around innocently, like maybe it's just raining inside, so he doesn't think you did the spraying.

Remember, though, that you have to catch your cat in the act.

Give kittens some leeway. There's a difference between a kitten's climbing behavior and destructive scratching. Kittens climb up on things because they're too small to jump very high. They'll outgrow this behavior within a few months, so you don't need to do anything about this except to cover expensive furniture for a short time and encourage real scratching on the post or pad.

The key to success is consistency. Everyone in your household needs to know how to use positive and negative reinforcement in training your cat where to claw. Children need to know this is not a game and not to use the water pistol for sport, at least not with the cat around. Your success will also improve the younger you start training your cat. It's best to start before six months of age. After six months, your cat will be training you!

Drew Weigner, D.V.M., is a board-certified specialist in feline practice and a diplomate of the American Board of Veterinary Practitioners. He is also a past president of the Academy of Feline Medicine. Dr. Weigner owns The Cat Doctor, a cats-only practice in Atlanta, Georgia. Visit Dr. Weigner's website at www.catdoctoratlanta.com.

Must-Know Info
From a Cat's-Eye View:
What People Do to Annoy Us

As a cat, I sometimes get treated as a second-class pet. I am pretty quiet about my needs, and I love my people. I just wish they would realize what they're doing—or not doing. I think they just don't know, mostly. So here are the top ten things that drive me crazy that I wish people would stop.

1. **They try to stuff me into a plastic cube they call a cat carrier.**

   Honestly, if they would just have started early by leaving the carrier out so I could use it for playtime or hiding, and better yet, if they would give me a few treats each time I went in, then I wouldn't mind so much going to Grandma's or the veterinary hospital.

2. **They yell at me for scratching the furniture.**

   Don't they understand that scratching is catly? Digging and stretching feels *so* good, and it's just my normal behavior for both claw care and for marking my territory. Maybe if they'd give me a nice sturdy scratching post that is tall and long enough, and showed me how to use it by putting catnip and playing with me there, then I would be happy to leave the sofa alone. Some other cat-friendly places to scratch, like those pads with corrugated cardboard, would be nice, too. And they could keep my nails trimmed or just ask the vet about trimming my claws. I *love* pedicures. Declawing me before I've even clawed anything isn't even fair. Ouch! Give me alternatives and teach me to use them. Is that so much to ask?

3. **They smoke.**

I suspect they'd like to quit. I've heard them talk about it. Maybe if they'd listen to what the veterinarians told them about secondhand smoke causing lung problems in cats, like asthma, they would at least start to cut back. Maybe their own doctor could help them quit.

4. **They put my only litter box in the basement by that noisy clothes dryer and ignore it.**

No wonder I don't use the box sometimes. I hate going down there, and the dog sometimes sits at the top of the stairs and doesn't let me go down. Plus, I don't like to share with my feline buddy, no matter how much I like him. But they never see that and just get angry if I can't get to that awful box. Besides, I'm getting a little creaky in my joints and going up and down steps each time I feel the urge is an inconvenience.

I wish they would realize we need one box per cat plus one extra, in different areas. At least one on each level, and they all need to be kept very clean. Leaving it dirty for days makes it pretty unpleasant. And then they wonder why I use the clothes hamper instead. Oh, and by the way, I'm not keen on fancy smells made for the human nose, either, so unscented litter is just fine.

5. **They give the dog really good monthly parasite pre-vention, but I only get some junk from the dis-count store that makes me feel all jittery.**

   Not to sound like a hypochondriac, but my health needs serious attention. I wish they would give me the prevention for heartworms and other parasites like fleas and intestinal worms—the stuff my veterinarian says works best and is safest for me. You know, if they ask, they might find out it's easier than they think to keep me healthy.

6. **They leave dry food out for days and expect that I will only eat what I need.**

   Hmmm . . . how long does that box of Oreos last in their cupboard? No wonder I'm pudgy and don't want to exercise and am getting even fatter. My vet tells them that I should get some canned food to help me stay hydrated—that's tough for us cats—and that they should measure the food to keep me from overeating. Get it right, or it'll be diabetes and the Catkins diet for me!

7. **They think a sedentary life is normal for me.**

   They say I'm lazy and aloof. Truth is, I've gotten pretty chunky, and I've developed arthritis. And because I don't limp like a dog on a walk, I just rest even more. Wow, and now I'm getting even fatter, which means I want to move around even less. Hello? Hello? Why won't they ask my veterinarian for help, so I can lose weight and be a normal, active cat? I'm built to move!

8. **They tell me I have stinky breath.**

   I wish they would realize how tarter on my teeth traps bacteria and eventually causes tooth and bone loss. And it hurts! If only they would quit thinking that giving me dry food helps my teeth, and take me to the veterinarian for help. After all, they go to the dentist every six months. I wish I would see the vet that often, and then the vet could tell them when I need to have my teeth cleaned so I could give them sweet kitty kisses.

9. **They buy toys for the dog, but not for me.**

   I am so sick of playing ugly stepchild to that dumb dog! I need toys, too. Lots of different ones. And hiding places like shelves and perches in the windows. These things keep me interested and active, and that helps keep me happy and healthy.

10. **They ignore me.**

   The absolute worst. What am I, a couch cushion? Well, they're wrong. I only want to be understood and loved in the way that I like, as a cat! If they want to get the most out of our relationship, they need to pay me some attention. Take care of me. Play with me. Pet me. Otherwise, I'm miserable. C'mon, people! Please get with the program. I love you!

Jane Brunt, D.V.M., is one of the leading feline practitioners in the United States and a recent past president of the American Association of Feline Practitioners. She has served in many leadership positions in veterinary organizations, including president of the Maryland Veterinary Medical Association. Dr. Brunt has coauthored articles in several peer-reviewed journals, served on numerous committees and panels to address feline issues, and addressed various feline matters in the consumer media. Dr. Brunt practices in Baltimore, Maryland, where she founded Cat Hospital at Towson (www.catdoc.com), an American Animal Hospital Association accredited practice and the first feline-exclusive veterinary hospital in Maryland. She opened a second practice, Cat Hospital Eastern Shore in Cordova, Maryland, in June 2001.

Must-Know Info
Feline Body Language

People are always saying cats are mysterious. Sure they are—especially if you can't interpret feline body language!

~~~~

Don't worry. You don't have to go through a language immersion course to learn to speak Felinese. You probably already know more than you think you do! With a little bit of knowledge and some careful observations, you'll soon understand your cat so well, you'll think Felinese was your first language.

Felinese has a lot to do with nonverbal cues—body language, in other words. To fully grasp your cat's mood, you have to observe not only her posture but her tail, ears, eyes, voice, and fur (including whiskers). A happy cat who is enjoying being petted from head to toe, for example, often arches her back to maximize contact with the stroking hand. On the other paw, a cat cornered by a potential attacker will assume the "Halloween cat" arched back. This kitty should be given wide berth. He's telling you, "Leave me alone and no one will get hurt." Ignore his advice and you're going to be sorry.

Frightened or angry cats hold their hair erect, hoping to look bigger and more intimidating; in the early stages of fear or aggression, some cats just puff out their tail. Whiskers have a broader repertoire in expressing emotion. If a cat is curious or angry, he holds his whiskers forward (cats also do this to "feel" their way around in the dark). Cats set their whiskers safely against their face when frightened.

Now, on to the small details that count a lot.

A cat's tail is one of the most reliable ways to tell his emotional state. A friendly cat will carry his tail upright and with the tip tilted slightly forward, especially if he's trotting toward the sound of the can opener. (Some cats in this frame of mind often appreciate being petted at the base of the tail and then being stroked along with the direction of the fur.) When he's holding his tail lower and puffier, he's telegraphing uncertainty—unless he's stalking, in which case it's low and stiffer, with a twitch at the end. A cat who's whipping his tail about is really unhappy. Tail-wagging may be a good thing in dogs, but in cats, it's a danger sign, and you'd better back off. The harder he thumps his tail, the shorter his fuse.

And what about the ears? Those beautiful fur-covered satellite dishes have an amazing range of motion—and each position of the ears means something different. A cat who's stalking prey— whether real or imagined—points his ears forward, listening for the tiniest rustle that will help him find what he's after. Once the game is over, a contented or happy cat will relax his ears as well. They'll still be up, but may be slightly to the side, and will flip around if any sound catches his interest. The ears you need to listen to, however, are those that are sideways or flattened against the head. These are the ears of a frightened or angry cat, and if you don't leave him alone, you may well find yourself nursing a bite or scratch.

A cat's eyes work pretty much on autopilot, reacting automatically to both changing light conditions and emotional states. Eyes that are opened wide but not so wide as to look "startled" suggest the polite interest of a relaxed cat. Wide eyes and large pupils suggest fear. A stalking cat (whether on the hunt for a mouse or a toy) has eyes that are open, "hard," and intensely focused. A cat who's ready to lash out narrows his eyes and focuses his pupils. By the way: Staring is never polite. Cats don't appreciate people gawking at them. They consider direct eye contact from strangers very rude, but with the people they love, they may share an "eye kiss." Catch your cat's eyes with yours and then slowly blink. Your cat may even blink back!

Some cats change emotional states very quickly, so watch for your cat's nonverbal cues indicating that he has had enough attention or grooming (or whatever you're doing to him). You can use your new knowledge of Felinese to help teach a poorly socialized cat to enjoy human contact. Quit petting or holding him before he gets antsy and you'll have him asking for more. By giving him treats and responding to his body language, petting can become a pleasurable experience for you both.

When petting a sensitive or skittish cat—or one you don't know well—stick to the cat's favorite areas—the ears, the cheeks, and the base of the tail. Watch to make sure the cat is happy and relaxed, and stop petting at the first sign of change, especially the tail and ears. Let him jump off your lap whenever he wants; otherwise, just sit quietly and watch. If the cat sticks around and relaxes, you can try a little more gentle affection. Treats won't hurt either.

Eventually, many nervous cats can learn to enjoy longer and longer sessions of petting—and from there, you can move on to brushing and other cat-maintenance tasks.

Dusty Rainbolt is an award-winning writer of many articles and books on cats, including *Cat Wrangling Made Easy: Maintaining Peace & Sanity in Your Multicat Home*, *Kittens for Dummies*, and *Ghost Cats*. She's the product editor for *Catnip* and writes columns and articles for *City+Country Pets*, www.stickypaws.com, and *Cat Fancy*. She keeps her herd of test kitties busy trying out the latest feline products. She has also raised countless orphaned kittens and fostered and placed over three hundred hard-luck cats. Her primary form of exercise is cleaning litter boxes, although she also scuba dives, which her cats understandably believe is certifiably nuts. Her website is www.dustycatwriter.com.

Must-Know Info

Must-Know Info
Shedding Solutions
for a Huggable Coat

Shedding is one of the top pet owner complaints. While people love their pets, they don't like dealing with the fur. Wearing your pet to work (on your clothes) is a badge of honor to some, but a nuisance to most. So how do you keep hair on the cat, off your clothing and furniture, and inside the trash? Moreover, how do you maintain a cat coat that's clean, soft, shiny, without mats, and parasite free, what some call "a huggable coat"?

Start by knowing what a great coat looks like. The ultimate cat coat is shiny, glowing, like a neon sign of sorts, a radiance that means inner health. And it goes without saying, no bare patches of skin (on a cat that's not supposed to have them!), mats, open sores, and foreign materials like plant seeds. If your cat has a dull, lusterless, or sparse coat, she has a skin or coat problem—or another illness.

But let's back up and talk about what you can and should do for your cat.

Most cats are low maintenance and take care of their own grooming. But some cats are prone to matting, especially those with a really fine undercoat like Persians and Himalayans. These cats need daily combing (not brushing), with equipment that gets right down to the skin. Many cat owners make the mistake of buying a slicker-type brush that only brushes the outer portion of the coat, leaving the undercoat to become matted. Cat owners need to pay particular attention to the cat's armpits, bib, tail base, and tummy, the very parts that some cats don't like touched. For a cat who's easy to groom, get your pet used to grooming early in life, working for short periods every day, using slow strokes, starting closer to the head where brushing is better tolerated. If you hit a matt, work it gently, making sure you don't pull the skin too hard. One hand holds the skin below the mat, and the other gently works the mat out.

All cats shed; some just shed more than others. While indoor cats who experience the same amount of light year-round may shed equally all year, there are two major seasonal shedding periods for cats who spend a lot of time outdoors. The cat's pineal gland responds to day-night (light) length, so we get twice-a-year shedding in most cats in the spring, to reduce the amount of fur borne through the cooler winter months and in the fall, presumably to get ready to grow a new coat.

Besides the natural shedding cycles, any disease affecting the skin or the hair follicles could affect the normal pattern of hair growth versus loss. Conditions in which increased amounts of hair are lost include malnutrition, ringworm (a fungal skin infestation), and other skin parasites living in/on the skin, including mites or fleas. And allergies can certainly increase hair loss due to inflammation of the skin. Overall ill health, malabsorption of nutrients, and hypothyroidism (rare) are a few examples of other things that can cause a poor hair coat and that may increase shedding.

Anxiety is a big cause for hair "loss." The hair is not actually *falling* out, but rather is being licked out; overgrooming is occurring that is often not witnessed by the caregiver. This is a "closet" behavior, performed when the owner is away or occupied by things other than interacting with the cat. The important difference is that the hairs remaining in the skin are broken off like a brush cut because of the barbs on the kitty's tongue, rasping the hair off, like sandpaper. The hair found in the home also has a barbered end rather than a nice, tapered point. When you tug firmly (but gently) on the hair, it is solid—it doesn't "fall out."

For all cats, rub your hands over their bodies on at least a weekly basis, checking for any unusual lumps or bumps that may indicate an abscess, tumor, foreign body, and so on. For a long-haired cat, combing and checking for mats at least once a week should be performed. For a short-haired cat, just check for mats and remove them when you find them. If you get your kitty used to being combed gently, it can be a pleasurable, bonding experience, and then daily combing is something you can enjoy together while it prevents mats from forming.

Monthly, trimming nails is a good idea. Check the base of the nail to see if there is any debris accumulating or redness of the skin. Redness of the skin around the nail would be a reason to seek professional advice, as nail bed infections can be very painful.

Regular combing and good nutrition maintain a healthy coat. Omega fatty acids have been shown to be beneficial for coat health. Finding the right balance of omega-3 and omega-6 is

important; many diets that are balanced and complete nutrition-
ally already contain this balance, so supplementation should not
be an automatic requirement for most cats. Some cats who have
particularly dull, dry coats may benefit from supplementation.
The best products are those that have been developed for cats,
not ones for humans, because the balance we need is different
from what a cat needs. Ask your veterinarian for a specific rec-
ommendation for a high-quality food that's best to put in your
cat's bowl, or if any supplements are recommended.

Along with combing, I recommend that my clients wipe their
kitty's coat after combing with a damp paper towel. This will pick
up the loose flyaway hairs and reduce the amount that ends up
being swallowed when kitty cleans her newly brushed coat, and
the amount of loose hair that will end up in the home or on you.
Some cats actually like being rolled with a sticky-tape lint roller.

Normal grooming results in ingestion of hair, including the
occasional hair ball. Regurgitation of hair balls more often than
two to three times a month is a sign of a problem. This could be
due to a gastrointestinal disturbance such as inflammatory bowel
disease, or from too much hair being ingested due to a skin irri-
tation or anxiety.

Most cats aren't particularly fond of water, and luckily for us and
them, cats rarely need to be bathed. Two exceptions to this are if
they are filthy (getting older and can't groom themselves as well
because of arthritis or oral pain) or have gotten into something you
do not want them to lick off themselves. Remember, when cats
groom themselves, they are ingesting whatever is in their environment on their coats as well as whatever they have walked through,

which may be simply gross (litter box contents), to toxic (particles from secondhand smoke), to deadly (antifreeze).

If you need to bathe a cat, you can do it without getting harmed or terrifying the cat (which is the reason you'd get harmed). Trim her nails first and place an artificial tear gel (ask your vet for some) in each eye before starting to help protect the eyes from soap. Do not try to place kitty into a tub or sink filled with water. Instead, place kitty in a dry tub/sink and use a handheld showerhead attachment (under $10 from the hardware store if you don't have one built in) with the flow directed on your kitty's body. Run low pressure, body temperature or slightly warmer water over the skin, top and bottom. Usually one hand is enough to hold the kitty in the sink. Then, using a shampoo specifically for cats (the right pH for a cat's skin and no chemicals that are toxic to cats), lather up and rinse, again, holding the showerhead right on the body. Towel dry (start by patting rather than scrubbing, as cats do not like to be "scrubbed") and comb out.

A shedding tool such as the FURminator can remove hair before it can be shed. You can also try using a spray static guard on furnishings and the lower part of walls/baseboards so that the hair doesn't stick. Of course, hardwood/laminate floors make cleanup with electrostatic, hair-grabbing products such as a Swiffer much easier.

Go into any veterinary hospital and you'll see that nothing beats the good old-fashioned sticky-tape roller. However, there are some new styles of these classic rollers that have a bigger surface and stickier tape. And there are some fabrics that don't hold hair as well as others: some of the Lycra mixes in clothing just drop the hair off; denim isn't bad, either. For furniture, we avoid anything with texture so that the kitties don't scratch it; again, slippery fabrics with a high sheen don't collect the hair as well.

Margie Scherk, D.V.M., is a board-certified feline special-ist, past president of the American Association of Feline Practitioners, and a consultant to the Veterinary Information Net-work. Founder of the Cats Only Veterinary Clinic in Vancouver, British Columbia (www.catsonlyvet.ca), Dr. Scherk has written dozens of papers and textbook chapters. She was selected the Canadian Vet-erinary Medical Association Practitioner of the Year for her work on using transdermal fentanyl patches and raising awareness regarding pain control.

Must-Know Info
Feline Introductions 101

Smitten with your kitten? That's as it should be. But maybe you already had a fur-kid or two, or now wonder about doubling the pleasure by adding another dog or cat to the mix. How well your current pet(s) will accept a newcomer depends on the age of animals involved, their health status, gender, genetics, and traits of instinct, size, personality—the list goes on and on. Informed pet choices and proper introductions make all the difference.

There are exceptions, but some dog breeds accept cats as buddies while others can be downright dangerous. Terrier types and sight hounds (Afghan hounds and greyhounds) may not be able to control their instinct to chase smaller critters, for example. Even a friendly eighty-plus-pound pooch could accidentally sit on and hurt your petite Persian.

By age twelve to eighteen months, your cat loses her inclination to make new cat (or dog) friends. She either attempts to get rid of any interlopers, or she hides and becomes a stranger in her own home. If resident pets had positive experiences with other pets as babies, they're more willing to accept a new buddy. This prime socialization period occurs from two to seven weeks for kittens and six to twelve weeks for pups.

As a general rule of "paw," it works best to choose a new pet that's younger than, and the opposite gender of, your resident pet. A baby doesn't threaten the adult's authority. This can work for dog-cat introductions, too. Dogs want to own "things," while cats want to own "space," so a young boy cat's desire for territory won't upset the resident female dog's preference for controlling all the toys.

It's not fair to introduce a new pet to *all* the cats and dogs in your household at once. Introductions should be done one pet at a time. Sometimes it's love at first sight, but more often, the pets take days or even weeks to learn to accept strangers.

Cat-to-Cat Introductions

Felines are the least forgiving of interlopers trespassing on their turf. Don't toss the new kitty into your existing clowder to "work it out," or you'll end up with the makings of a slasher film! Think of it this way—how would you like being forced to share your dinner plate, toilet, and bed with a funny-smelling stranger off the street?

Respect your resident cat's prior claim to territory. Confine the new kitty in a single room by herself, so the resident cat understands only *part* of his territory has been invaded. This also keeps the new cat more comfortable by providing a familiar safe retreat.

Provide a litter box, food and water bowls, toys, scratch post, and other kitty paraphernalia in the new cat's room. Keep the door closed for at least the first three days—a week or longer may be required, though. Watch for sniffing and paw pats underneath the door. Expect normal posturing, fluffed fur, and hissing, and when that begins to fade, you're ready to go to the next step.

The cats should "know" each other by scent before they ever set eyes on each other. Felines identify their family group by a communal scent created by mutual grooming and sleeping together, so use this sense as a powerful tool during introductions.

After each cat has a meal, switch out the plates temporarily so that they can sniff bowls and become even more familiar with each other. It's even better when a bit of food is left, because that helps the cats identify good stuff—food—with the other animal.

After several days, give the new cat a chance to scope out the rest of the house for a couple of hours. Kitties have no interest in meeting new people or pets unless they feel comfortable with the environment. Segregate your current feline in another room, then open the door so the new cat has private time to cheek rub (scent) furniture and find good hiding and sleeping places. If you can manage it, your resident cat can be exploring the "safe room" at this time, too, to become more familiar with the new kid.

Finally, you're ready for a nose-to-nose meeting. Don't make a big deal of this: simply open the "safe room" door, stand back, and watch what happens. Remember, the first face-to-face between cats should be one pair at a time, so if you have more than one resident cat, confine the others until a private meeting is possible. Introduce the friendliest resident cat to the newcomer first, so they have a chance to form a bond and can offer a positive example to the others who can copycat the behavior.

Be prepared to stop any all-out altercations (toss a towel over the top of them), but allow hissing as long as the cats keep their distance. Distract them by feeding or playing a game at the same time, but on opposite sides of the room.

Some cats take to each other right away, while others require days, weeks, or even months to accept somebody new into the family. Help the pair smell alike by rubbing a sock over the cheeks of the resident cat first and then over the new cat's body.

Until you are satisfied no fur will fly, keep the new cat in her safe room whenever you can't supervise the cats. A baby gate in the doorway (try stacking a couple) can allow safe interactions but keep them safely separated.

Cat-to-Dog Introductions

Nearly half of all pet families in this country include both cats and dogs in the household. These very different animals appreciate each other as family members, but only if correctly socialized to each other as infants and then properly introduced.

Dog-to-dog introductions are best begun on "neutral" territory such as a park. But cats aren't willing to meet anybody until they are familiar with their environment, so an off-site meeting won't work. Compromise by introducing the pets in your home, with accommodations made to the sensitivities of the cat and dog involved.

When bringing a new dog into a cat's home, have a friend do the "dirty deed" out of the cat's sight (if possible), so your cat won't associate you with the "scary" critter. If the new pet is a cat, though, send your new dog outside of the house and let him see you carry the cat crate inside, so he knows his human leader approves. He won't make as big of a fuss if he finds your cat already in the house.

Confine your new pet (cat or dog) in a single room, door closed, with all the necessary accoutrements. Include the new guy's favorite bed or toy, so the old, familiar smells help keep him calm. Isolating the new cat or dog tells your resident pet that not all of the house and territory has been invaded.

Cats normally posture or hiss while dogs typically sniff, whine, growl, or bark at the closed door. Feel encouraged once the barking and hissing fade, especially if the canine "play bows" at the door or the pair play patty-cake paws under the door.

Once a few days have passed and the growls or hisses fade, swap items that each pet has scented, so they have a closer sniffing opportunity to get acquainted. For instance, bring out the food bowl each has emptied to allow the other critter to smell.

When the new kid is a cat, she'll need an opportunity to wander around the rest of the house and become comfortable with her surroundings. Remember, cats aren't interested in meeting new friends until they know all the good hiding places and have cheek-rubbed and mapped the territory. Send the dog into the yard during the cat's exploration, or shut the dog inside of the new cat's room, so he can sniff where she's been.

Install a baby gate in the isolation room, so the pets can see and sniff each other and meet at their own speed, but through the safety of the barrier. Look for confidence and interest, and if either pet shows shyness or aggression, keep the gate in place for another few days.

When you finally open the barrier, let the pets interact at their own speed. Keep your dog on a leash to help him control his enthusiasm, and be sure your cat has access to "high ground" to get out of doggy nose range if needed. Help both pets associate good things with each other's presence by feeding them at the same time on opposite ends of a room. For play-oriented pets, engage them in separate games during the first meetings.

Use scent to speed up acceptance. Dogs and cats smell alike when they are friendly because they sleep together and share a familiar "family" smell. Dab a bit of your favorite cologne on the back of the neck and base of the tail of both animals to help the dog feel better about the cat. The product Feliway, an analogue of the cat's cheek pheromone, can reduce kitty stress by helping the cat feel better about her environment. Feliway comes as a spray or plug-in.

Until you are satisfied the pets accept each other, keep the new guy in his "safe room" when you cannot directly supervise. Take your time and practice patience during introductions. Proper introductions ensure your cats and dogs enjoy their future together, in your very own peaceful kingdom.

Amy Shojai is a certified animal behavior consultant and a nation-ally known authority on pet care and behavior, spokesperson for the pet industry, and author of twenty-two pet books. Her award-winning columns appear in the *Herald Democrat* newspaper, CatChow.com, Pet-Side.com, HomeAgain.com, and www.ivillage.com. She hosts a twice-monthly TV *Pet Talk* segment at KXII-CBS, the weekly *Pet Peeves* show at PetLifeRadio.com, and is the "Pet Guru" for the WeSeed.com investment and social networking site. Amy addresses a range of fun-to-serious issues covering dogs and cats, and is a popular speaker on pets and writing. Her books include PETiQuette: Solving *Behavior Problems in Your Multipet Household* and the bestselling *Chicken Soup for the Dog Lover's Soul* and *Chicken Soup for the Cat Lover's Soul.* She and her husband live with Seren(dipity) the Siamese wannabe, Magic the German shepherd, seven koi, and other assorted critters at Rosemont, their thirteen-acre spread in north Texas. Learn more about Amy's work at www.shojai.com.

> # Must-Know Info
> ## Getting Beyond the "Achoo"
> ## in Your Relationship
> *From The Ultimate Coauthors*

Allergies to cats aren't caused by fur, but rather by an element called "Fel d 1" found in cat saliva and urine. When a cat shakes or rubs on items—or uses the litter box—that allergen gets distributed everywhere. Here are some tips to help minimize the problem.

Work with an allergist. Allergies and asthma are serious health problems, but more allergists today are willing to help you keep your cat and maintain your health.

Establish your bedroom as an "allergy-free zone." Make the bedroom completely off-limits to pets at all times. Minimize other allergy triggers in your bedroom according to your allergist's guidelines.

Limit exposure to other allergens. If possible, get someone else to mow the lawn, do the vacuuming, and clean the litter box. If you can't avoid these tasks, wear a mask and wash your hands immediately afterward.

Keep your cat clean. Weekly bathing of your cat in clear water is a must—it keeps down the dander levels. Putting the litter box into the garage may help as well.

Must-Know Info
Start Your Sponges: Get on Pet Messes Right Away
From The Ultimate Coauthors

Speed is key when dealing with pet mess. Catch messes quickly and you reduce any possibility of staining. Another good reason for addressing pet mess promptly: urine and feces smells tend to attract "repeat business," making it more difficult to house-train a kitten or cat and tempting already house-trained pets to regress.

If the mess is fresh, you can use a gentle dish soap, putting a teaspoon or two into a quart of warm water along with a teaspoon of vinegar. Start by picking up and disposing of any solids. Blot the area with towels, then wet it with the cleaner. Let it sit for a few minutes and then flush with clean water and blot, repeating a couple of times to make sure the soap is removed.

Older but still fairly recent messes are more difficult to deal with. Use an enzymatic cleanser designed for pet stains, following the directions on the label. These products break down the organic compounds in the mess, helping it to let go of the fibers of carpet or upholstery.

Resources

American Animal Hospital Association (AAHA), 12575 W. Bayaud Avenue, Lakewood, CO 80228; 800-252-2242; www.healthypet.com

Established in 1933, the American Animal Hospital Association is the only organization that accredits veterinary practices throughout the United States and Canada for dedication to high standards of veterinary care. More than three thousand AAHA-accredited practices pass regular reviews of AAHA's stringent accreditation standards, which cover patient care, client service, and medical protocols. For pet care information or referral to an AAHA-accredited practice, visit www.healthypet.com.

American Society for the Prevention of Cruelty to Animals (ASPCA), 424 E. 92nd Street, New York, NY 10128; 212-876-7700; www.aspca.org

Founded in 1866, the ASPCA aims to prevent cruelty and alleviate the pain, fear, and suffering of animals by providing local and national programs that assist thousands of animals nationwide. The ASPCA's national programs include the Animal Poison Control Center, humane education, companion animal services, and national shelter outreach.

American Veterinary Medical Association (AVMA), 1931 N. Meacham Road, Suite 100, Schaumburg, IL 60173; 847-925-8070; www.avma.org

Founded in 1863, the AVMA is one of the oldest and largest veterinary medical organizations in the world. Its more than seventy-six thousand member veterinarians recognize the importance of the human-animal bond and the veterinarian's role in preserving, protecting, and strengthening relationships between people and animals. AVMA members contribute to the health and well-being of people and animals through work in clinical practice, public health, regulatory agencies, uniformed services, and research.

Animal Behavior Resources Institute (ABRI), P.O. Box 27348, Golden Valley, MN 55427; 612-209-1578; www.ABRIonline.org

ABRIonline.org provides free training and behavior resources to companion animal professionals and their clients. Resources include videos, podcasts, interviews, articles, and research studies featuring leading veterinarians, behaviorists, trainers, and other professionals. The ABRI's mission is to enhance human-animal relationships and improve the quality of life for people and animals by providing high-quality education and animal-behavior information.

Cat Fanciers' Association (CFA), 1805 Atlantic Avenue,P.O. Box 1005, Manasquan, NJ 08736; www.cfa.org

Founded in 1906, the CFA is a nonprofit organization that maintains the largest registry of pedigreed cats in the world and is the governing body for more than four hundred shows internationally. The organization also supports animal disaster relief and advocates for better knowledge of care for all cats.

Delta Society, 875 124th Avenue NE, Suite 101; Bellevue, WA 98005; 425-679-5500; www.deltasociety.org

The Delta Society's mission is to improve human health through service and therapy animals. The organization works to expand awareness of the positive effects animals can have on human health, reduce barriers that prevent the involvement of animals in everyday life, and expand the therapeutic and service role of animals in human health, service, and education. Delta Pet Partners volunteers visit hospitals, nursing homes, schools, hospices, and other facilities with their pets, providing animal-assisted activities and therapy throughout the United States and the world. The Pet Partners program registers all types of pets, including dogs, cats, rabbits, birds, horses, and other domestic animals.

The Humane Society of the United States (HSUS), 2100 L Street NW, Washington, DC 20037; 202-452-1100; www.humanesociety.org

The HSUS is the nation's largest animal protection organization, and it supports building and enhancing the human-companion animal bond through its Pets for Life campaign. Pets for Life provides solutions to behavior issues; restrictions on rental housing and the concerns of allergic, pregnant, or immuno-compromised individuals; and promotes humane animal care and adoption to end the relinquishment, abandonment, and euthanasia of healthy dogs and cats.

Morris Animal Foundation (MAF), 10200 East Girard Avenue, Suite B430, Denver, CO 80231; 800-243-2345; www.MorrisAnimalFoundation.org

Established in 1948, the MAF is dedicated to funding research that protects, treats, and cures companion animals and wildlife. MAF has been at the forefront of funding breakthrough research studies benefiting animals in some one hundred countries, spanning all seven continents on Earth. MAF has its headquarters in Denver, Colorado. The Foundation has funded nearly 1,400 humane animal health studies with funds totaling more than $51 million.

PetConnection.com, www.PetConnection.com

The online home of Dr. Marty Becker, "America's Veterinarian," and his writing partner, Gina Spadafori. The two are syndicated columnists and top-selling pet-care authors. Together with other members of the PetConnection team, they offer pet lovers a free, searchable library of top-quality pet medical and behavior advice, as well as other resources, including newsletters and contests for pet lovers. The PetConnection.com web log is the pet lover's must-go daily check-in for the latest in pet health and animal advocacy news. PetConnection.com's affiliated site, Dog-Cars.com, offers free reviews of new vehicles and travel advice for dog lovers.

Winn Feline Foundation, 1805 Atlantic Avenue, Manasquan, NJ 08736; 732-528-9797; www.winnfelinehealth.org

The Winn Feline Foundation was founded by the Cat Fanciers' Association (CFA) in 1968 to create a source of funding for medical studies to improve cat health and welfare. CFA continues to be actively involved by providing invaluable office, publication, and meeting support. Winn has funded over $3 million in health research for cats at more than thirty partner institutions worldwide.

The Writers

Sabrina Abercromby is a freelance writer. Her work has appeared in *Cat Fancy, California Garden, San Clemente Times*, and many other publications. She lives in Southern California with her husband, Keith, and their two cats, Felix and Gabriel, who have filled their home with joy, laughter, and lots of cat fur.

Liz Blackman, inspired by her own two rescued dogs, Lita and Winchell, founded 1-800-HELP-4-PETS, an identification system that works like a nationwide 911 service for pets in any emergency—lost, home fire, car accident, natural disaster, and travel emergencies. Since 1996, 1-800-HELP-4-PETS has helped thousands of pets get help and get home. For more information, listings for lost and found pets, and advice on how to prevent loss and find a missing pet, visit these websites: www.help4pets.com and www.TheCenterForLostPets.com.

Jane Brunt, D.V.M., is one of the leading feline practitioners in the United States and a recent past president of the American Association of Feline Practitioners. She has served in many leadership positions in veterinary organizations, including president of the Maryland Veterinary Medical Association. Dr. Brunt has coauthored articles in several peer-reviewed journals, served on numerous committees and panels to address feline issues, and addressed various feline matters in the consumer media. Dr. Brunt practices in Baltimore, Maryland, where she founded Cat Hospital at Towson (www.catdoc.com), an American Animal Hospital Association accredited practice and the first feline-exclusive veterinary hospital in Maryland. She opened a second practice, Cat Hospital Eastern Shore in Cordova, Maryland, in June 2001.

Isabel Bearman Bucher and her husband, Robert, continue their honeymoon with life. In January 2008, they adopted a little dog, Maisie, from the Animal Humane Society—their first dog in over twenty-five years. The also enjoy their eldest daughter's three adopted stray cats. Isabel began yet another adventure, developing a website where her first book, *Nonno's Monkey: An Italian American Memoir* can be found. She's made it a home to begin geneology searches, write a family recipe book, travel info, and more. Many stories from the memoir can be found in past Chicken Soup for Soul anthologies. Enjoy her work at isabelbucher.com.

Cindy Buck coauthored *Chicken Soup for the Gardener's Soul* and was a contributing editor of many other titles in that series, including *Chicken Soup for the Cat & Dog Lover's Soul*. She lives in Fairfield, Iowa, where she edits nonfiction books and for years hosted a weekly radio program called *That Pet Show*. Cindy can be reached at cbuck@lisco.com.

Tony Buffington, D.V.M., Ph.D., diplomate of the American College of Veterinary Nutrition, is a professor of veterinary clinical sciences at The Ohio State University Veterinary Hospital. Dr. Buffington is world-renowned for his expertise on pet nutrition, and for his interest in the health of indoor cats. The Ohio State University

College of Veterinary Medicine created the Indoor Cat Initiative to enrich the lives of indoor cats, in the belief that indoor enrichment is as important to cats' welfare as an excellent diet and health care. Learn more about Dr. Buffington's work on his website at www.indoorcat.org.

Rick Capone lives in Lexington, Kentucky, with his little buddy, Rascal, an orange tabby mix who works very hard to live up to his name. Rick has been writing for over twenty years and currently works for the American Volleyball Coaches Association as editor of *Coaching Volleyball* magazine.

Vanni Cappelli is a freelance journalist who has covered conflicts in the Horn of Africa, the Balkans, and Central Asia since the early 1990s. He is the president of the Afghanistan Foreign Press Association.

Rachael Carpenter, D.V.M., is a clinical assistant professor of anesthesia and pain management at the University of Illinois College of Veterinary Medicine. She is also a consultant to the Veterinary Information Network. She has worked as an emergency and critical care veterinarian and did her internship at the prestigious Rood and Riddle Equine Hospital in Lexington, Kentucky.

Beth Cato counts books and cats as her closest companions. She is married to Jason and is a stay-at-home mother to their son, Nicholas. Beth is from Hanford, California, but now dwells in the desert outside of Phoenix, Arizona.

Diane Ciarloni lives in Texas with a houseful of dogs, cats, rabbits, and birds and a barn full of horses. She is a professional freelance writer with works appearing in several national anthologies. Diane is also the author of *Legends*, a special-interest book about horses. You can contact her by e-mail at eaglesrest@centurytel.net.

Robin Downing, D.V.M., is a pain management consultant and lectures internationally on the importance of preemptive pain management in the compassionate care of companion animals. She is the current president of the International Veterinary Academy of Animal Pain Management and is one of only five veterinarians in the world to hold the diplomate credential in the American Academy of Pain Management, the largest interdisciplinary pain management organization in human medicine. In 2001 the World Small Animal Association presented Dr. Downing with the Excellence in Veterinary Healthcare Award (Small Animal Veterinarian of the Year). She is also an accomplished and popular writer on pet and veterinary issues. Dr. Downing serves as a trustee for the Morris Animal Foundation and is an affiliate faculty member at Colorado State University's College of Veterinary Medicine. She is also a certified veterinary acupuncturist and a certified canine rehabilitation practitioner, having trained at the University of Tennessee College of Veterinary Medicine.

Susan Farr-Fahncke is the founder of 2TheHeart.com, where you can find more of her writing and sign up for an online writing workshop. She is also the founder of the volunteer group, Angels2TheHeart, the author of *Angel's Legacy*, and the co-author, editor, and contributor to more than fifty books, including many in the

Chicken Soup for the Soul series. She welcomes you to visit her at www. 2TheHeart.com.

Lisa Finch graduated with honors from McMaster University with a B.A. in English. Her writing has been published locally and in the recently released anthology *Living the Serenity Prayer* (Adams Media). She lives in Forest, Ontario, with her husband, Chris, and their three children, Hailey, Matthew, and Ben. They have two adored cats, Bella and Hemingway.

Mitzi Flyte is a registered nurse who has been writing since she was twelve, when her equipment of choice was a Royal portable typewriter, and her office was her family basement. Since then she's written personal essays, short stories, poetry, feature articles, and opinion pieces for the local daily newspaper. She lives in Easton, Pennsylvania, with three furry companions and is working on a paranormal mystery series. Visit her website at www.mitzimusings.blogspot.com or e-mail Mitzi at mitzi.flyte@gmail.com.

Jack Frye is retired from the U.S. Navy and is currently performing aircraft maintenance for the U.S. Air Force. He is a widower living with four bottle-fed rescued cats, Gilligan, Sophie, and Bridget, who are four years old, and Marty, who is two; and one ten-year-old Siamese named Itch.

Jeanna Godfrey, D.V.M., graduated from Texas A&M University College of Veterinary Medicine in 1980 and has been in private practice for twenty-eight years. She lives in southern Texas with her husband, Larry, and three remarkable cats: Pgme (pronounced "pig me," which stands for "possum got my eye"), Billy Bob (known as Willy Billy or Love Chicken), and PuttPud (convinced he's reincarnated royalty). Dr. Godfrey is equally enamored of horses and was a contributing writer for *Chicken Soup for the Horse Lover's Soul II*, as well as the author of the book *How Horses Learn*, available through major online booksellers or at www.backinprint.com.

Mary Lynne Hill, Ph.D., lives with her husband Andy, son A.J., and Molly the cat on a farm in Fort Worth, Texas. A former tenured professor at St. Mary's University, she now is an independent scholar, writer, and civic engagement consultant. Her website is http://web.mac.com/marylynnehill.

Teresa Hoy's passion for animals began as a small child. While other children played with dolls, she played with stuffed animals. A writer, freelance editor, and paper artist, she divides her time between her computer, her art studio, and caring for the large fur family she and her husband have adopted over the years. Visit her at www.teresahoy.com.

Roberta Beach Jacobson (aka The Cat Lady) is a humorist and author who blogs at http://blog.seattlepi.nwsource.com/catlady. A member of the Cat Writers' Association and the National Society of Newspaper Columnists, she makes her home on a tiny Greek island. It's the sort of remote spot where animals outnumber people.

Nancy Edwards Johnson writes stories and memoirs of growing up in the Blue Ridge Mountains of Virginia. She's been a longtime contributor to area magazines and has written a monthly column for *Latitude Magazine* in Winston-Salem, North Carolina, for over two years. Her e-mail address is nancyedwardsjohson@yahoo.com.

Dolores Kozielski is a certified feng shui consultant practicing in New Jersey. She is an author, artist, and award-winning poet and has published with major publishing houses, including HarperCollins. Dolores is a contributor to *Chicken Soup for the Soul Healthy Living: Stress, Chicken Soup for the Sister's Soul 2, Chicken Soup for the Beach Lover's Soul,* and *Chicken Soup for the Coffee Lover's Soul.* Dolores can be reached at www.fengshuiwrite.com.

Bettina Kozlowski is a writer, freelance journalist, and multimedia producer in Chicago. Her published magazine articles range from features about Tajikistan, to rebuilding New Orleans after Katrina, to profiles of pop stars. Bettina was born in Poland and grew up in Germany. She has also lived in London, Paris, and Los Angeles, where she worked in TV and feature film development. If you would like more information about Touched By An Animal, a unique organization dedicated primarily to preserving the bond between the elderly and their companion animals visit www.touchedbyananimal.org.

Gary Landsberg, D.V.M., is board-certified in veterinary behavior both in North America and in Europe. In addition to his general veterinary practice, Dr. Landsberg offers behavior consultation services at the North Toronto Animal Clinic. He is a frequent speaker on behavioral topics at veterinary conferences around the world and has coauthored a number of veterinary behavioral texts as well as a series of behavior brochures. Dr. Landsberg has also hosted his own TV and radio shows. He was awarded the American Animal Hospital Association award for his contributions to the field of companion animal behavior and is a past president of the American College of Veterinary Behaviorists. His website is www.northtorontovets.com.

Jennifer Larsen, D.V.M., Ph.D., is a board-certified veterinary nutritionist and clinical nutritionist with the Nutrition Support Service at the University of California Davis Veterinary Medical Teaching Hospital. She is also a consultant to the Veterinary Information Network and a member of the Scientific Advisory Board, Davis Veterinary Medical Consulting.

Suzanne Thomas Lawlor's passion is inspiring people through her writing, coaching, and teaching. Suzanne, her partner, and Gracie, who Suzanne is convinced is more angel than feline, live in the beautiful Oakland hills of Northern California. Suzanne can be reached at riverofgrace@aol.com.

Susan Little, D.V.M., a board-certified feline specialist, is the president of the Winn Feline Foundation (www.winnfelinehealth.org). She serves on the editorial advisory committee of *PETS Magazine* and is a consultant for the Veterinary Information Network. Dr. Little is a contributing author to several publications, including *The Cat Fanciers' Association Complete Cat Book* (2004) and the Royal Canin *Practical Guide to Cat Breeding* (2005), as well as several veterinary journal articles. She is a peer reviewer for the *Journal of Feline Medicine and Surgery* and the *Canadian Veterinary Journal.* She is also an internationally known lecturer on feline medicine.

Gregg Mayer is a former dancer, choreographer, and arts professional who has worked extensively in Europe and the United States. She now teaches yoga, Pilates, and meditation and is the founder of All Sentient Beings, Inc., in New York City. Gregg can be contacted at www.angelfire.com/ct3/wellbeings77.

Judy Merritt has been writing for thirty years and is currently working on her third novel. She is an editor/reporter for the *Northwoods Press* in Nevis, Minnesota, where her four cats allow her to live in their home.

Judi Moreo is the author of the award-winning book, *You Are More Than Enough: Every Woman's Guide to Purpose, Passion, and Power* and the companion, *Achievement Journal*. She is a motivational speaker who resides in Las Vegas with her kitties, Shotsie and Brut. Judi can be reached through her website, www.judimoreo.com.

Amy Mullis lives in the foothills of South Carolina with husband, Bill, sons Ryan and Jeffrey, and assorted animals who have stopped to smell the bacon and decided to stay. Amy was named humor columnist for thewahmmagazine.com, an e-magazine for work-at-home parents. Read more of her work in *Chicken Soup for the Beach Lover's Soul*, *Chicken Soup for the Chocolate Lover's Soul*, and on her blog at www.mindovermullis.blogspot.com.

Lucyann Murray is a freelance writer and artist currently employed as a correspondent for a Chicago newspaper. Lucyann is a native of Chicago but has lived in northern California most of her life. Love of animals is one of the wheels that keeps the world turning for her.

Susan Boskat Murray is an independent writing contractor whose work appears often in *The WORLD of Professional Pet Sitting*, a publication of Pet Sitters International. She received the 2008 Florida Christian Writers Conference First Time Conferee "Best Work" Award. Sue shares her home with her husband, three college-age offspring, one dog and sixteen felines.

Arnold Plotnick, D.V.M., a board-certified small animal internist and feline specialist, is the founder of Manhattan Cat Specialists (www.manhattancats.com), a full-service, feline-exclusive veterinary facility located on the Upper West Side of New York City. Manhattan Cat Specialists' goal is to continue to advance the cause of feline medicine.

Felice Prager is a freelance writer from Scottsdale, Arizona, with credits in local, national, and international publications. In addition to writing, she also works as a multisensory educational therapist with adults and children who have moderate to severe learning disabilities. For a sampling of her essays and contact information, please visit her website, Write Funny! at http://www.writefunny.com.

Dusty Rainbolt is an award-winning writer of many articles and books on cats including *Cat Wrangling Made Easy: Maintaining Peace & Sanity in Your Multicat Home*, *Kittens for Dummies*, and *Ghost Cats*. She's the product editor for *Catnip* and writes columns and articles for *City+Country Pets*, www.stickypaws.com, and *Cat Fancy*. She keeps her herd of test kitties busy trying out the latest feline products. She has also raised countless orphaned kittens and fostered and placed over three hundred hard-luck cats. Her primary form of exercise is cleaning litter boxes, although she also scuba dives, which her cats understandably believe is certifiably nuts. Her website is www.dustycatwriter.com.

Margie Scherk, D.V.M., is a board-certified feline specialist, past president of the American Association of Feline Practitioners, and a consultant to the Veterinary Information Network. Founder of the Cats Only Veterinary Clinic in Vancouver, British Columbia (www.catsonlyvet.ca), Dr. Scherk has written dozens of papers and textbook chapters. She was selected the Canadian Veterinary Medical Association Practitioner of the Year for her work on using transdermal fentanyl patches and raising awareness regarding pain control.

Amy Shojai is a certified animal behavior consultant and nationally known authority on pet care and behavior, spokesperson for the pet industry, and author of twenty-two pet books. Her award-winning columns appear in the *Herald Democrat* newspaper, CatChow.com, PetSide.com, HomeAgain.com, and www.ivillage.com. She hosts a twice-monthly TV *Pet Talk* segment at KXII-CBS, the weekly *Pet Peeves* show at PetLifeRadio.com, and is the "Pet Guru" for the WeSeed.com investment and social networking site. Amy addresses a range of fun-to-serious issues covering dogs and cats and is a popular speaker on pets and writing. Her books include *PETi-Quette: Solving Behavior Problems in Your Multipet Household* and the bestselling *Chicken Soup for the Dog Lover's Soul* and *Chicken Soup for the Cat Lover's Soul*. She and her husband live with Seren(dipity) the Siamese wannabe, Magic the German shepherd, seven koi, and other assorted critters at Rosemont, their thirteen-acre spread in north Texas. You can learn more about Amy's work at www.shojai.com.

Troy Snow is a professional freelance photographer whose work has been widely published and appreciated. Along with a team from Best Friends Animal Society, he went to the Gulf Coast in the aftermath of Hurricane Katrina to help animals and people. The stories from that rescue effort are told by his stunning photos in the book *Not Left Behind: Rescuing the Pets of New Orleans*. Many of snow's photos are on the Best Friends website (www.bestfriends.org), and you can see more of his work at www.troysnowphoto.com.

B. J. Taylor loves sprawling out in the sunshine with Red. She is an award-winning author whose work has appeared in *Guideposts*, many Chicken Soup for the Soul books, and numerous magazines and newspapers. She has a wonderful husband, four children, two grandsons, one dog, three cats, and one fish. You can reach B. J. through her website at www.clik.to/bjtaylor.

Sandra L. Toney has been writing about cats for fifteen years. An award-winning author and photographer of eight books, such as *The Simple Guide to Cats* and *The Little Book of Cat Tricks*, Toney is a professional member of the Cat Writers' Association. She lives in Indiana with her husband and three spoiled felines.

Susan Tripp and **Rolan Tripp, D.V.M.**, have followed their hearts into a career helping people develop better relationships with their pets. Dr. Tripp, an affiliate professor of applied animal behavior at both Colorado State University and the

University of Wisconsin, has lectured on animal behavior around the world. He is also the principal veterinary consultant to Petmate, one of the largest manufacturers of pet products in the world. Susan Tripp is a writer, speaker, and teacher who shares her husband's passion for developing kinder, gentler experiences for pets in veterinary practices and at home. The Tripps write *On Good Behavior* for the Pet Connection syndicated newspaper feature. For more information, visit www. AnimalBehavior.net.

Sue Vogan is a published author, book reviewer, and radio show host.

Janet Vormittag is a freelance writer who lives in western Michigan. She publishes *Cats and Dogs*, a free magazine that promotes spay/neuter and the adoption of animals from shelters and rescues.

Samantha Ducloux Waltz's essays can be found in the Chicken Soup for the Soul series, Cup of Comfort series, and a number of other anthologies. She has also published adult nonfiction and juvenile fiction under the names Samantha Ducloux and Samellyn Wood. She lives in Portland, Oregon.

Drew Weigner, D.V.M., is a board-certified specialist in feline practice and a diplomate of the American Board of Veterinary Practitioners. He is also a past president of the Academy of Feline Medicine. Dr. Weigner owns the Cat Doctor, a cats-only practice in Atlanta, Georgia. Visit Dr. Weigner's website at www.catdoctoratlanta.com.

The Photographers

Sabrina Abercromby is a freelance writer. Her work has appeared in *Cat Fancy, California Garden, San Clemente Times,* and many other publications. She lives in Southern California with her husband, Keith, and their two cats, Felix and Gabriel, who have filled their home with joy, laughter, and lots of cat fur.

Sarah K. Andrew is one of the most exciting and talented young equine photographers to debut in years. In the last few years, Sarah and her camera have become well known at New York and New Jersey racetracks and other equine sport venues. Her work has been published in many publications, including the *New York Times,* and hangs proudly on many a horse owner's wall. For more information, visit her at www.RockandRacehorses.com.

Amanda Borozinski is a full-time reporter and photographer for the *Keene Sentinel,* a daily newspaper in Keene, New Hampshire. Her work has appeared in *Guideposts* magazine, *Positive Thinking* magazine, TheHorse.com, the *Northern New England Review,* the *Oklahoma Review,* and the *Boston Globe.* In 2008, she was awarded a fellowship from the prestigious MacDowell Colony, and spent three secluded weeks working on an upcoming book project. Amanda can be reached at aboro@ptcnh.net.

Jennifer Crites is a Honolulu-based photographer and writer whose words and images of travel, contemporary lifestyles, and science have been published in magazines and books worldwide. Her first love, though, is photographing our furry, four-legged friends. She invites readers to visit her website at www.jennifercritesphotography.com to see more pet portraits.

Sharon Fibelkorn is a freelance photojournalist known for her keen eye and refined editorial work. She specializes in action photography. As a working photographer, her pictures have added visual illustration to most of the top publications throughout the world, both as editorial content and advertising. But it's those intimate portraits that grace personal homes and barns that have a special place in her soul. To simply say she enjoys taking a picture isn't enough. To say she has enjoyed her journey in life while creating and living moments with her subjects would be a better statement.

Zachary Folk, based out of Seattle, Washington, specializes in portrait photography. His online galleries are updated with samples of his past work photographing dogs, children, and business head shots. Zachary also maintains a photoblog to organize his travel photography and daily shootings. For questions about scheduling and prints, please send an e-mail to zachary@folkphotography.com. To see Zachary's work, visit his website at www.folkphotography.com.

Ryan Hutchinson is an amateur photographer from Halifax, Nova Scotia, Canada. Ryan's main interests in photography lie in wildlife, motorsports, and waterfalls. He is always working to improve his photographic skills. Ryan's photography can be enjoyed at www.Ryan-Hutchinson.com.

Laura Layera is originally from Toronto and is now a professional photographer based out of Los Angeles. While she shoots mostly portraits and weddings, she's an unabashed animal lover and takes pictures of animals every chance she gets. Her favorite subject is her cat, Mister Peaches, who is a feral rescue from the streets of Los Angeles. You can e-mail Laura at luluphoto@gmail.com and visit her website at www.luluphoto.com.

Nancy McCallum enjoys photographing all kinds of animals, specializing in cat, dog, and horse photography. Nancy's images can be seen in a wide range of publications, including calendars, books, and magazines. Nancy finds inspiration in nature and enjoys relaxing on the family farm in Michigan, finding and photographing the extraordinary in the ordinary. She is constantly adding to her collection of images. Visit her website at www.mccallumphoto.com.

Norman Rehme holds master's degrees in photography and photographic craftsman. He photographs a wide variety of subjects from infants to the elderly, landscapes to animals. Some of the most popular models for him now are his grandchildren. Norman collaborates with his author wife, Carol. The photo of the orange tabby that appears in this volume is from a lazy summer afternoon in central Kansas on a farm. It was taken with a Nikon D200 and a 24–120mm lens. Please visit Norman and enjoy more of his work at www.rehme.com.

Troy Snow is a professional freelance photographer whose work has been widely published and appreciated. Along with a team from Best Friends Animal Society, he went to the Gulf Coast in the aftermath of Hurricane Katrina to help animals and people. The stories from that rescue effort are told by his stunning photos in the book *Not Left Behind: Rescuing the Pets of New Orleans*. Many of snow's photos are on the Best Friends website (www.bestfriends.org), and you can see more of his work at www.troysnowphoto.com.

Maggie Swanson, a freelance illustrator of over one hundred children's books, lives in Connecticut with her husband, Rick, and two exceptional cats, Tommie and Gracie. Enjoy her work at www.maggieswanson.com. She volunteers at PAWS animal shelter. Many of her photographs are of cats who passed through the shelter on their way to new homes.

Lynn Tait is a widely published poet and an amateur photographer from Sarnia, Ontario, Canada. She began by taking photos while traveling on the back of her husband's motorcycle. One of her photos will be on the cover of a poetry anthology, *Sounding the Seconds* in the summer of 2008. You can e-mail Lynn at lyta@sympatico.ca.

Angelina Wilson is a freelance writer based in a small town along the Ohio River where she lives with her cat, Thomas, and other pets. Thomas spent his first year of life exploring the stable where Angelina boards her horses. He'd "help" her clean stalls by riding in the wheelbarrow and by perching on her shoulder. Nowadays, though, he's happy exploring around the house and watching nature from the screened-in porch.

The Authors

Marty Becker, D.V.M., is the regularly featured vet on *Good Morning America*, a frequent veterinary contributor to *The Martha Stewart Show*, and the host of the PBS series *The Pet Doctor with Marty Becker*, which airs in hundreds of markets nationwide. He coauthored the *New York Times* bestseller *Why Do Dogs Drink Out of the Toilet?* and *Chicken Soup for the Dog Lover's Soul*. He has appeared on Animal Planet and writes a syndicated pet-care feature for newspapers across America and Canada, syndicated through Universal Press. Often called "America's Veterinarian," he has been named Companion Animal Veterinarian of the Year by the Delta Society and the American Veterinary Medical Association. Dr. Becker lives in Bonners Ferry, Idaho.

Gina Spadafori is the author of an award-winning weekly column on pets and their care, which is syndicated through Universal Press. She is a bestselling author of several pet books, which have sold 375,000 copies combined, including the *New York Times* bestseller *Why Do Dogs Drink Out of the Toilet?* and *Dogs for Dummies*. The first edition of *Dogs for Dummies* received the President's Award for the best writing on dogs by the Dog Writers Association of America. She has served on the board of directors for both the Cat Writers Association of America and the Dog Writers Association of America. Gina lives in Sacramento, California.

Carol Kline is a freelance writer and speaker and the bestselling coauthor of five books in the Chicken Soup for the Soul series, including *Chicken Soup for the Cat Lover's Soul* and *Chicken Soup for the Dog Lover's Soul*, as well as other books on a variety of topics. An animal rescue volunteer for years, Carol is affiliated with Noah's Ark Animal Foundation in Fairfield, Iowa.

Mikkel Becker received her degree in intercultural communications from Washington State University. Mikkel has been active in the Quarter Horse show circuit, and she is a three-time Canadian National Champion in Western Pleasure and Hunter Under Saddle. Mikkel is a contributing author to Knight Ridder newspapers, *Cat Fancy* magazine, and *Chicken Soup for the Soul*.

C:.pyright Credits

(continued from page ii)

Index

Every cat needs a good place to sit, think, and scratch.

The beauty of a cat is
best shown, not told.

You know what they say,
"Big hair, big heart."

In every cat, in every spot and
stripe, there is always the
reminder of the wild.